MAKE MEN STRONG AGAIN

THE 12 PILLARS OF TRADITIONAL MASCULINITY

ASHMAN
FREE PRESS

COPYRIGHT

ISBN: 978-1-7360306-7-7 (Author Special Edition Hardback)
ISBN: 978-1-962192–01-9 (Hardback)
ISBN: 978-1-7360306-8-4 (Paperback)
ISBN: 978-1-7360306-9-1 (eBook)
ISBN: 978-1-962192-00-2 (Audio)

FIRST PAPERBACK EDITION DECEMBER 2023

CREDITS

Creative Director - Brian Giles
Design by - Jesse Hopkins Design
Illustrations by - Gabriel Sorondo
Indexed by - Michael Hendry
Edited by - Bryan Alexander, Gareth Collinson, Brian Niemeier

Ashman Free Press
Boston, MA
ASHMANFREEPRESS.COM

Growing Stronger is about accumulating wisdom, learning from your mistakes and inspiring others to become The Strongest Version of Themselves.

- ELLIOTT HULSE | YOUTUBE @YoElliott

TABLE OF CONTENTS

INTRODUCTION i

Why I'm Writing This Book ii
The 12 Pillars of
Traditional Masculinity iv
Who This Book Is For vi
Who I Am vi
How This Book Is Organized viii

LIFT 1

1. Your Moral Duty to Be Strong 2
2. LeBron James and the Role Player 3
3. Grab That Axe 4
4. Girls, Money, and Bill Gates 5
5. The Four Big Exercises 6
6. Get Started Lifting 8

READ 11

7. Don't Waste Energy Reading 12
8. Burn Your Books 14
9. Read About Religion 15
10. Arm Yourself with History 16
11. Guard Against Subversion 17
12. Communist War Against Catholics ... 18
13. Your Mom Lied to You 19
14. Books on Fapping 20

STOP 23

15. Addiction to Pleasure 24
16. Battle Against Your Demons 26
17. Learn From the Church Fathers 27
18. Enter Monk Mode 29
19. The Fire Of Lust 30
20. Don't Argue With The Demon 33
21. Ask For Help 34
22. Pray 35

FAST 37

23. I Didn't Know I Had Demons 37
24. How to Get Clarity in Life 39
25. Survive the Zombie Apocalypse 40
26. Autophagy 41
27. Five Powerful Ways Fasting
    Helps Your Body 41
28. Burn Fat Not Muscles 42
29. Stop The Traffic in Your Body 44
30. Respect Our Ancestors' Way of Life 45
31. Philosophers Weren't Always
    Frigging Bookworms 47

OPTIMIZE 49

32. The Unpopular Truth About Estrogen
    & Testosterone 50
33. How to Make Your Heart
    Health Strong 52
34. Leaders, Leaders, Leaders 53
35. Your Testosterone Level Is Falling ... 54
36. Testosterone Danger 55
37. Remove Plastics 56
38. Natural Ways to Optimize
    Testosterone 57

DEFY 59

39. It's Okay To Be The Villain 60
40. The Warrior Child 61
41. Become Intolerant 62
42. Say No. 63

DEVOTE 67

43. The King's Crown 67
44. It's Going to Fall Apart 68
45. When I Quit 69
46. The Ultimate Cause 69
47. Beyond Reason 70
48. You're Gonna Hate Me 71
49. Acknowledge and Accept
the Flaws 72
50. Don't Cut and Run 73

REVEAL 77

51. The Slap of God 78
52. Waiting For Mommy to Tell Us 79
53. Look for God's Pattern 79
54. Allow It to Unfold 81
55. Start with the Man in the Mirror 81

ACT 85

56. Don't Light a Candle and Hide It 85
57. The Ugly Bonobos 87
58. Don't Be Active —Take Action 88
59. Sit Down And Relax 89
60. Troll Goal Trap 91
61. Soul Goal Method 93

GUARD 97

62. Watch Over Your Holy Soul 98
63. Violent Sexual Revolution 100
64. Disorienting Information 101
65. Why We Are Confused 102
66. Guard Against Programming 102
67. My Sin 103
68. Two Bad Personality Types 104
69. Women Are Stomping on
Our Necks 105

CREATE 109

70. The Generative Principle 110
71. Ride the Wave 110
72. Create With God 110
73. Resistance Is a Clever Demon 111
74. Let Resistance Be Your Guide 112
75. Stay Stupid 113
76. Stay Stubborn 114
77. How Will It Unfold? 115

BE 117

78. You Will Have a God 117
79. The Trump God 118
80. You've Been Sold a Paper Boat 118
81. Save Your Soul 119
82. Chop Wood & Carry Water 120
83. Save the World 122
84. The Story of Rabbi Zusha 122
MASSIVE ACTION PLAN 125
SPECIAL OFFER 126
You Should Follow Me Here 127
Index 128-136

INTRODUCTION

INTRO

It's time for you to become the strongest version of yourself, and in this short book, I will show you exactly how to do that, making use of the incredibly powerful methods of traditional masculinity.

When you finish reading this book, you will be well on your way to achieving self-mastery, conquering your vices, and developing your virtue. You will learn how to fully unleash your inner strength—that same strength which our degenerate society tries so hard to keep apart from you. Ultimately, you will be able to build more muscle, make more money, and be with the girl of your dreams.

There are twelve pillars of traditional masculinity which make men strong that we'll go over. The first pillar is *lifting*, because when you're working with me, it all starts with strength. It's difficult for a man to be mentally strong if he's physically weak. Personally, of late, I've been doing a lot of Farmer's Carries, which is cool because I live on a farm now, and do them with my son. Atlas Stones are also amazing, and I'll always love them, since I was a professional strongman. But the truth is, you don't need anything complicated to build an immaculate body and get stronger than most everyone you know. I will cover four simple yet incredibly effective exercises that will quickly get you strong. We will also go over the general importance of strength in your life.

Being physically strong is great, but it's only a start. A man also has to be mentally and spiritually strong. That's why in this book we will go deep into the mindset of strength, and do so by focusing on traditional masculinity. Why is that? It's because traditional masculinity is so powerful. We are not after some New Age fad or quick fix that won't actually work. The techniques, advice, and ideas in this book will truly make you a stronger man.

This book will hopefully be especially useful to you, because we not only go over the wisdom of traditional masculinity, but also apply it to the unique problems men face in our degenerate world today. For example: How important is testosterone for men and why do feminists hate it? How should you respond when demons are attacking you through Instagram? Is it possible to be masculine when our culture systematically hides mortality from us?

Those are just a few of the dilemmas that men face nowadays. We're going to go through them, and many more, to identify the dangerous obstacles that our degenerate world lays out there, that can slow you down and stop you from achieving your full potential, and apply the lessons of traditional masculinity to unleash the power inside of you.

WHY I'M WRITING THIS BOOK

The simple fact is that boys are no longer taught masculine values. It used to be different. Those masculine values were just a part of the simple facts of life. Boys used to work in farming, riding horses, and literally hunting wolves. Males were rewarded for their feats of masculinity.

Nowadays, it's a different story. Boys sit at desks all day being harangued by feminist teachers, while men get smeared and denigrated in the media, books, and movies. Society relentlessly bashes any display of masculinity.

It's not a pretty sight when a man meekly accepts this sad state of affairs. His inner strength dissipates, and into that void comes rushing all these awful values: effeminacy, modernism, degeneracy, gynocentrism. There's a lot to unpack here and throughout this book we'll be taking a close look at these ideas and the dangers they pose to you. For instance, we'll get into how gynocentrism has mentally blocked men from *guarding* themselves against women degrading them. We'll also look at the incredible philosopher, Saint Thomas Aquinas, and his warning against effeminacy.

We'll have to leave the explanation at this, though, for the introduction: These are terrible and damaging ideas. They will make your life worse. If you pick up these ideas and behaviors, then you do real damage to yourself and to your loved ones. You will lose the respect of others. You will lose your own pride. You will become lost in life.

Trust me, it's a painful place to be. I've been there. Further ahead in this book, I will share some of my rough experiences when I got trapped in effeminate ways. But just to reiterate, it's awful. If you're there, it's time to get out, right now. If you're not there, do everything you can to make sure you never get in that place, and strengthen your connection with like-minded men.

So here is the answer to the question above and my

explanation about why I'm writing this book: It's because nowadays, using the power of traditional masculinity to become the strongest version of yourself, takes conscious effort. It takes thought, conversation, reading. We have to fight back against the dangerous inertia in our degenerate culture, otherwise men can lose their innate masculinity without even realizing it, and that is just unacceptable. This book is for men who want to take advantage of their God-given power as men.

THE 12 PILLARS OF TRADITIONAL MASCULINITY

Inside this book are the ideas that are proven to work, based on my thousands of hours working with men, that will get you real-life results too. I can tell you that I teach similar concepts in my King Initiation program, working with a tight-knit group of growth-minded men, and the results these men have are almost unbelievable: They blast through barriers to dominate their lives.

The twelve pillars of traditional masculinity that we will cover are: *Lift, Read, Stop, Fast, Optimize, Defy, Devote, Reveal, Act, Guard, Create, Be.* These are ideas that successful men intuitively understand and live by. They used to be commonly accepted, but these days, it's a different story, and they've become a lost wisdom, almost a type of hidden lore, or secret.

Even worse, when they haven't been outright lost to us, they're talked about in the mainstream for the sole purpose of smearing them. They try to gaslight us into forgoing our

God-given rights and duties. That's why I'm writing this book. The problem is a huge one, so my pushback here is extreme. This book is an alarm clock for your soul. I'm excited to go over the ideas of traditional masculinity with you.

Many of the ideas in this book you won't easily be able to find anywhere else. *Lift* may be the only one that most people know about, but even then, it's one thing to learn about strength training from an entry on WebMD, and another to learn about it from someone who won strongman competitions. We are talking about developing full-body strength and why it's important to do so.

Optimize is one I really enjoy. That's where we will talk about the importance of testosterone and optimizing it for our well-being. There are serious myths surrounding a man's testosterone. Society tries to bully you into disrespecting your own testosterone. We get into that, and I explain why testosterone is important, and push back against the lies of our anti-man culture.

Another great pillar that we're going to go over is *Devote*. Many men are confused nowadays because they *devote* themselves to unworthy causes, often without even realizing it. So we're going to explore why it's so important to find a worthwhile cause to *devote* yourself to, what that means, and how you can *reveal* that cause to yourself. I love these twelve pillars. So many great truths in here.

Eventually we build up to the final and greatest pillar, *Be*. This is where we learn to confront our mortality and be the strongest version of ourselves. As you may have guessed from the name of my King Initiation program, my work revolves around building up our inner king, and though this book takes a different angle on it, we go over related ideas here. We are building ourselves up as men. That means physical, mental, and spiritual strength, so that you can protect and provide for yourself and your loved ones, and have success in life.

WHO THIS BOOK IS FOR

This book is not written for women. It's also not written for men who respect effeminate society the way it is and have no desire to improve their own lives. Here is who this book is actually for: men who value strength and masculinity, want to become the best versions of themselves, gain control over their lives, and merit the respect of women, family, and loved ones.

No matter where you're at in life, there will be value in here for you. Some men feel lost, and in that case, this book will help you to quickly conquer your problems and get back on the path. Other men are doing well in life, but want to do even better, and in that case, this book will get you excited and may help to challenge and strengthen your values. I love working with all you guys.

WHO I AM

Before we start the book, I need to briefly tell you who I am, so that you know who you're dealing with. My name is

Elliott Hulse. My clients call me the King of Making Men Strong. I'm Catholic, a master strongman, strength coach, and father figure to millions of men worldwide. I have over two million YouTube subscribers, almost all of whom are men. Not only do I teach them how to be physically strong, but I also show them how to be stronger men in their lives.

My work didn't just change my life, it also changed my family's life. I'm a husband and father of four. A few years ago, I was able to move my family to a cattle ranch in rural Florida, where we're homesteading and homeschooling our four children. I also helped my Mom and Dad to retire and live in the country. That's something I always wanted to do.

But my world wasn't always this great. Early in my career, I suffered several devastating injuries and setbacks. As a result, I fell into a trap that many men find themselves in at some point. I allowed myself to become extremely emotional, growing out my hair, and smoking marijuana.

Due to my indiscretions, I lost almost everything: strength, wealth, fame, friends, and I almost lost my family.

The final straw came after a dream I had. I received the message that my father-in-law and myself were about to make my wife miserable. The following day, her father died. This was the wake-up call that inspired me to discover the root cause of my own weaknesses and the hidden reason behind most men's failure today. What I discovered blew my mind. I discovered what it takes for any man to overcome effeminate flaws and to become the kind of strong and masculine leader that women and the world at large need us to be.

HOW THIS BOOK IS ORGANIZED

This book is for you, the reader. There is no time-wasting crap in here. I'm making this book short and to the point. That means, we have short chapters and easy-to-use sections inside of the chapters. This is so that you can actually read and enjoy the whole thing.

The idea of this book is to get you real results. There is no energy-draining intellectual rambling in here. This book is full of ideas you can actually take action on. Please feel free to start from the beginning and read to the end, or if some part calls to you in particular, skip right to it. Use this book to build the strongest version of yourself.

The only thing you will find in here is pure, traditional masculinity, that will get you thinking, excited, and help you to unleash your power.

A life without pain is a life without challenge,
a life without challenge is a life without growth.

BONUS & EXTRAS

Throughout this book there will be links to supplemental content online, providing an in depth discussion about various topics.

This Bonus and Extra material, along with any updates, will be available at:

MAKEMENSTRONGAGAIN.COM/BONUS

MAKE MEN STRONG AGAIN FREE VIDEO COURSE

Every pillar in this book stems from an in-depth video course which over **3,000 MEN paid $997** for.

With the purchase of this book, this transformative journey, that is encapsulated in **12 Powerful Videos**, is now **My Gift To You** at **NO CHARGE**.

Discover the depth behind each pillar by visiting here:

MAKEMENSTRONGAGAIN.COM/12PILLARS

LIFT

Every man carries the weight of the world on his shoulders, from the weight of frustration because he can't find a job, to the weight of lethargy from not being able to sleep at night with that newborn baby, to the weight of rage for that chick who betrayed him even though he gave his heart. Worst of all is the weight of carrying the fact that you know you're not living up to the strength that is within you, and not being the strongest version of yourself.

All of this pressure accumulates. It grows so heavy that your body feels like it's going to break. So what does a man do when he feels like he's on the brink of destruction? What does a man do when he feels like the weight has become unbearable? He learns to lift. He learns to lift because of who he can become.

And when you discover that all the challenges in your life are just like the plates that you put on the barbell—your jerk boss, broken heart, the sick baby—and that each one of them is designed specifically to strengthen weaknesses within your character, then that's when you learn not only to accept these challenges, but to beg for them. *Lay your heavy burden on my shoulders, so that I can grow stronger. Bring it on.*

1. **YOUR MORAL DUTY TO BE STRONG**

Women will never be as strong as men. It will *never, ever, ever, ever* happen.

Here's the truth. If a woman can beat the crap out of you, well, that makes you less of a man. Sorry, it might sound politically incorrect, but it's true. Of course, this isn't the case in every single situation. Sure, okay, there are some MMA chicks out there who would beat my ass. But I'm talking about in general. Like my wife—she can't be stronger than me. She will never be stronger than me. No matter how hard she trains, no matter how many steroids she takes, it doesn't matter what she does, she will never be able to overpower me.

A woman will never be able to overpower you, unless you let her.

God gave you the gift of being the stronger sex. That's a fact. Strength is a masculine competence. It's what allows us to hunt. It's what allows us to work. It's what allows us to forage and dig and drag and push and pull and do all the things that we can do. Why not take full advantage?

That also means that man is the provider and, really, has to be the provider. There is no other way. It's in our bone structure, the strength of our muscles; it's in our genes, and in our testosterone. And deep down, everyone knows it's true. It's easy to see the truth of this fact in a funny meme that's out there. It has a woman in one frame who says, "Women can do anything that a man can do." In the next frame, she's looking out the window at six feet of snow and a guy is out there shoveling snow over his shoulder. Then in the final frame she says, "Just not right now." No one is confused about this joke's meaning. Everyone gets it.

All this has to be considered when looking at why it's men who rule the world. Nowadays, women think they rule. This causes confusion, gets into men's heads, and we can forget the basic truth of the situation. So it's important to remember—and again, this is just a fact—there is nothing women get in this world that men don't allow them to have. Nothing. That women have gotten so much is simply because men give it to them.

The point here isn't to knock women. I have three daughters, a wife, and I love women. But this world has disempowered and emasculated men to a tremendous degree. So the purpose of my work is to make men strong again. We are uplifting men here.

2. LEBRON JAMES AND THE ROLE PLAYER

There's a level of authority that comes with a man's strength, and with that authority, there is also responsibility. Responsibility will always lie with who is strongest. It doesn't matter if this is a family, an organization, a company, or a sport. The idea is the same. When the Lakers don't win, everyone wants to know how LeBron James was playing; no one really cares if role player number eight got his two rebounds that game. Likewise, when it comes to the family, final responsibility lies with the dad. It's a man's moral duty to be strong. You've got to protect. Can you? Do you have confidence in your ability to protect those close to you and fend off attackers?

3. GRAB THAT AXE

A basic level of strength is important, a requirement even, to handle basic life problems.

I live in Florida, and down here we get hurricanes. If a tree falls down in our driveway, and we can't get our cars out and the emergency vehicles can't get here, and I'm not in shape, then we're in trouble. If I'm strong, then we can handle it. If I'm not, then we're screwed.

I need to know that I'm strong enough so I can grab a saw and start sawing that dead tree up myself. I'm going to move those logs out of the way. My wife can't do that, she wouldn't be able to, and my children are still too small. You know what Big Daddy does? He uses that saw, even if it's a manual saw, and Big Daddy goes out there and he gets it done. Grab that axe. Right? Grab that axe, get out there, and get it done.

It goes beyond just being able to get the job done. It's also about the confidence you get from knowing you can, should the problem arise. There is no substitute for the mental strength you gain from strength training. Competence and confidence are something that people can sense about you. It's in the aura you put out. It's in the way you walk, the way you talk, and the look in your eyes. You can see and sense it in some people right away. Their character just exudes it.

That confidence gets embodied and shows up as strength. You need to look like the type of man that you aspire to be. Some people say that looks don't matter: "Don't judge a book by its cover." But I don't believe that. I'm telling you right now, looks do matter and people do judge a book by its cover.

Now, you don't need to be a bodybuilder, but there's no reason to be weak. All the information and inspiration that you could ever need—to build a strong character, strong body, and strong posture—is available to you right now.

By the way, while some people may think that strength is only for young men out chasing girls, that's not the case. That's wrong. A man always needs strength. Whether you're single or married, young or old, strength is important. In fact, it may actually get more important as you get older, because that's when it's easier to get soft, lose muscle, put on weight, and feel lethargic. Testosterone levels go down. So, yes, it stays important to lift and gain strength, to counteract Father Time.

It's always important for a man to be strong. So that we can grab that axe and dominate a problem.

4. GIRLS, MONEY, AND BILL GATES

Here are yet more reasons to lift: status and attraction.

Women are attracted to physically strong men. It's called polarity. While they may date and marry men who are weak, that's not because of attraction, it's only because of pragmatics. They marry someone like Bill Gates because he has money. There is even something "attractive" about him in the way he "flexes" his brain. He's got status and owns a corporation. But when he's walking down the street in his sweater, are girls really smelling his pheromones? Nope. They're not checking him out. They're not turning their heads, they're not looking at him as an alpha male who walks with confidence and posture, or even just looks tolerable.

This is true even if some women say otherwise. Women often say things they don't understand or even know why they're saying it. They may even genuinely think it's true. But they just don't know. You really need to listen less to what women are saying and look more at what women are doing.

Regardless of what women say, they are always far more attracted to hard and muscular men. So that's another benefit to lifting. It's going to lead to attraction and create that natural polarity.

5. THE FOUR BIG EXERCISES

I'm going to share the four best exercises. You can literally design a training program for years around variations on just these four lifts and develop a big, strong, athletic, good-looking body.

The first exercise is the deadlift. The deadlift will help you to develop an incredibly strong and good-looking body. It's the simplest of all movements—you just lift the bar off the floor. But it's not the easiest lift, because you've got to make sure that your body is set up properly. In order to deadlift properly, everything from your neck and head, down through your shoulder girdle, into your core and hips, and down to your legs, knees, and feet, need to be working well. You can't have significant dysfunction anywhere in your body and have a strong deadlift. That's why you can spend years developing a huge deadlift, which also means addressing any dysfunction that is holding your deadlift back, and you will become the strongest version of yourself by that alone. Understand the importance of working on the deadlift.

The second exercise I'm going to give you is an upper body exercise: dips. They develop the chest, shoulders, and triceps. There are so many different ways to adjust the parameters with the dip. You can add weight by hanging a chain from your hips. You can play with the tempo by adding in pauses or going slower to add more time under tension. Dips are going to build thickness, strength, and flexibility. You know, part of the reason why a lot of people can't do dips is because their shoulders are damaged due to poor posture. Like I said with the deadlift, if you spend time improving your dip, it doesn't just mean you only do tons of dips, you've got to go back and fix all the messed-up muscles so that you'll be able to maximize your dip.

Next come front squats. I've done entire videos on YouTube just on how powerful these are. They force thoracic extension, which will make you strong and healthy. Beyond that, you're developing your core, because if you don't have a strong core, let me tell you, that bar is just going to fall onto the ground. If you've never done heavy front squats before, go ahead and try them, then you'll see what I mean about working your core. Front squats are yet another one of those exercises that you won't be able to do well with dysfunction in your body. These things help you develop your posture, they require ankle mobility, a strong core, and more. More so than the deadlift, they're going to work the front of your legs, namely your quads. This is full-body training that will give you amazing strength and health.

Finally, we have chin-ups. Different variations of pulling your body up to a bar. This is just the basics here and it's the best training ever. Pulling yourself up to a bar is what we've had to do since the dawn of mankind, climbing trees, climbing cliffs, doing what we had to do to survive. It's going to develop your biceps, your rear delts, and more. It may even improve your sprinting speed. This is another self-limiting exercise. You can't fake good chin-ups.

Boom. Right there. These four exercises will give you the best results ever. Deadlifts, dips, chin-ups, and front squats. You can design a great program and build an immaculate body with just these four exercises.

6. GET STARTED LIFTING

You need to be able to produce maximal strength. That's true whether you want to jump high, run fast, or just look good. Above, we introduced some of the best exercises, but it also helps to have a concrete training program to work with. I am a big fan of 5X5. That's a great training program that works well for just about anyone, whether you are a beginner, intermediate, or advanced lifter. There's something in there for everybody. It has a good, moderate workload, so you're not burning yourself out, but you're definitely getting real strong. Then I did my own advanced 5x5 program with my own take on it. Finally, there's also "Starting Strength" here, which is sometimes favored more for beginners.

THE PROGRAMS

- **Starting Strength -**
  Basic programming to get started.

- **Bill Starr 5x5 -**
  Well-rounded program to get anyone stronger.

- **Elliott Hulse Advanced 5x5 Variations -**
  The classic program with some twists to maximize your gains, includes detailed explanations and breakdowns.

BONUS

For additional details on the
workout programs visit:
MakeMenStrongAgain.com/BONUS

Strength is not just about muscle; it's the foundation of a man's courage, resilience, and the ability to shoulder life's burdens.

READ

Read deeply and widely. This is an idea that will come up throughout this book. Whether you're trying to improve your lifting technique, unravel the lies of our degenerate world, or study the teachings of Jesus Christ, reading is crucial.

A big inspiration to me personally was Ralph Waldo Emerson. He is the author of the famous essay "Self-Reliance," which, by the way, I encourage you to check out because it's very powerful and very cool. He was a renowned lecturer who toured lyceums and gave well over a thousand talks. And he was known for being a reader—maybe one of the greatest readers in history.

By the age of fourteen, he was a student at Harvard, where he studied Greek, Latin, and rhetoric. He did that all while working to support himself. Later on, he completed Divinity School.

He read a truly massive amount. He read the classics of ancient Greece and Rome, the Bible, other historical Christian books, classic works of literature from Europe and England, as well as contemporary books and magazines. But he didn't stop there. He also studied Buddhism, Confucianism, Hinduism, and even Zoroastrianism. He read scriptures from the East, Norse mythology, and books on botany. He even read government papers like the "Annual Report of the Commissioner of Indian Affairs, 1849."

To be self-reliant, and to confidently go down your own unique path in life, you have to read. That's how you get knowledge and develop your ideas. When you are working to get good at something, whether that be your job as a strength trainer, or in sales, or as a dad, include reading in that process. Read a lot, and read widely.

7. DON'T WASTE ENERGY READING

Merely reading isn't enough though. You need to be an active and selective reader. If you read everything and anything that comes your way, you're going to waste a lot of your time. Beyond that, you will even do real damage to yourself, if you are passive and don't discriminate between which written words you allow to penetrate your mind.

You have to read the right way. Pay attention to what you're reading, and only read what is useful, helpful, and enjoyable to you. Throw away the rest.

Look at what Emerson did. Even though he was one of the best-read men of history, he didn't mindlessly consume everything. He was a very discriminating reader, and quite thoughtful about how and what he read. Here are some of the great guidelines he offered:

EMERSON'S GUIDELINES

1. **Don't waste time on daily news**
   "Transfer the amount of your reading day by day from the newspaper to the standard authors."

2. **Obey your internal compass**

   "[Young men] grow up in libraries, believing it is their duty to accept the views which Cicero, which Locke, which Bacon have given, forgetful that Cicero, Locke, and Bacon were only young men in libraries when they wrote those books."

3. **Take action on what you read**

   "Action... is essential. Without it, [the scholar] is not yet man. Without it, thought can never ripen into truth."

4. **Protect your time and energy**

   "Learn how to get *their* best too, without their getting yours. Do not read them when the mind is creative. And do not read them thoroughly, column by column. Remember they are made for everybody, and don't try to get what isn't meant for you... There is a great secret in knowing what to keep out of the mind as well as what to put in."

■ ■ ■

That's how I approach reading. I use a gold highlighter and it's funny because it's like I'm mining the book for gold nuggets. The fact is, I don't want to remember or even to see everything in a book. I just want the good stuff. Maybe only ten percent of it is worthwhile. Sometimes, I buy a book and only read a single chapter, the rest of it I just spit right out. Emerson took out lots of books from the library, but he didn't read them all. Don't stress out over not finishing every book. It's not a problem.

8. BURN YOUR BOOKS

People assume it's always good to read more, but that's not the case. Sometimes it's going to hurt you, and that even includes reading good books. Here's the reason and why it can be a problem: You can get addicted to knowledge. It seems obvious when talking about knowledge in the context of TikTok or scrolling on Instagram or YouTube, but the basic idea holds true even for books.

If you become a glutton for information, then you will hurt yourself. The same way you can grow obese from eating too much food, your mind can grow sluggish from reading too much. Information, if used in the wrong way, can become a crutch, and it can even become toxic. It's an inflammation of the mind.

Occasionally, we have to take the challenge of cutting ourselves off from too much information. That means cutting off the news, cutting ourselves off from social media, cutting ourselves off from information and even from books.

Look at what Nietzsche wrote, and this was back when there were orders of magnitude fewer books than there are today: "The scholar, who in sooth, does little else than handle books... ultimately forgets entirely and completely the capacity of thinking for himself... in him the instinct of self-defense has decayed, otherwise he would defend himself against books."

We're not only talking about screening out bad books, we're also talking about worthwhile books. Even those can become a problem for our minds. Too much worldly knowledge can be the mark of effeminate pleasure-seeking and we can easily become prideful. I know because I've grown very prideful at various times due to the number of books I've read. So I went ahead and did a book detox. I threw away over half of my books.

Books are a tool, and like any tool, you can hurt yourself if you use them wrong.

9. READ ABOUT RELIGION

You have to understand the foundations upon which Western Civilization was built, and that means learning about Christianity. It's true that the Church hasn't always been perfect; nevertheless, the spread of Catholicism gave us a more or less virtuous society, where you can trust your neighbor to not kill your family and steal your wife. You cannot be a Western Man and not know the Bible. This doesn't mean you need to become super religious, but it is important to at least read about the history.

Everyone has an opinion on the Bible nowadays, in this world we live in, dominated by atheism, communism, and feminism, but a lot of those opinions are just hatred and propaganda. I myself had all sorts of opinions about the Bible until I actually read it. That's how I discovered that the Bible is the most red-pilled book on the planet. That's actually why most people hate it. The Abrahamic religions are patriarchal, and that's to our benefit as men. Religion was created by men and for men—women are tapped into something different—but it was men who recognized we needed this patriarchal authority, from above, from God the Father, to lead us right.

When I was younger, I was attracted to Buddhism, Hinduism, and Taoism. I was into all that stuff. But that's just how it had to be for me to come full circle, back to Christianity. Only now can I see the value in it and get the food I was searching for. Only now can I see the beauty in Biblical writings.

So, if you want to be a virtuous Western Man, then really focus some energy here. Read the history of the Church. If you have an aversion to Christianity, which our atheistic world usually instills in us, maybe get started with the writings of the early Church Fathers. Those guys read like Taoism and Zen, they were hooked in, they were monks. And read the Bible.

10. ARM YOURSELF WITH HISTORY

Humans are easily led astray. This is especially true in our decadent world. There is a war on our minds coming at us from so many angles.

Defend yourself with history. Because when there is no history, then there is no wisdom, and without wisdom, how can you stay true to yourself?

Look at the writings of James Baldwin, who was an African-American writer from the 1950s. He grew up in a tumultuous time and wanted to figure out what was going on. So he dove deeply into the history of African and European people. He found that African civilizations did not have much in the way of written culture. Having a written history is a mark of an advanced civilization, so he lamented that African people didn't have that written history. He tried and he searched but couldn't find anything that he could relate to. So he got into European history.

If you're American, European, white, black, Hispanic, mixed, from the Middle East, Muslim, or if you're just simply here in America—then know the history of the West. Study it. Dig deep. Look outside the realm of the typical self-hating lies that we learn in school. Find something of value. Find something for yourself.

11. GUARD AGAINST SUBVERSION

If you want to destroy a people, take their real history away, and force a fake history on them. That's what's happening in America, and as a result we are losing our culture. But we have to fight back against that and guard our cultural inheritance. Sometimes you have to dig really deep just to get to the truth because our histories have been fabricated and perverted to such a huge extent. This is a matter of being a seeker in terms of history and culture.

As a first-generation American, this point resonates with me in a special way. My parents taught me to love America because they grew up in squalor in Belize. They came here because they wanted something better, and so I've learned how to love and appreciate American culture.

But we're losing our love of America and all things American. We've been losing it for a century because there has been an issue there. The West is being lost to subversion by communists. This was highlighted in a famous talk, when a communist defector gave warning about the Kremlin's massive campaign of ideological subversion. He explained the main vector of Communist attack: "[is to change] the perception of reality, of every American, to such an extent, that despite an abundance of information, no one is able to come to sensible conclusions in the interests of defending themselves, their families, their communities, and their country."

We see the results around us every day. It helps to have the willpower to fight back but that is only a part of it. To get through the fog of their lies, reading the facts of history is important.

12. COMMUNIST WAR AGAINST CATHOLICS

Communists have targeted many entities for destruction, from America, to the family, to classical education. But many are unaware that they have specifically targeted Catholics. This can make it very hard today for Catholics to live and remain proud Catholics. There is an undercurrent of hatred and lies directed towards Catholics and it's important to understand the history of how that came about.

The Kremlin saw that the Church was a centralized point of resistance in favor of morality, tradition, and God, and against Communism. So they decided to devote enormous resources specifically into tarnishing the Church.

There's a lot going on here, but here's an example to give you an idea of how this process of Communist attack on Catholics works in practice.

Back in the 1960s, there was a play called "The Deputy," which portrayed Pope Pius XII as complicit with the Nazis. On the surface, it appeared to be a play created by men in the West, as the producer was German, the writer was German, and it was released in Western Europe. That's what the public saw and accepted. But behind the scenes, the play had been written by the KGB, and only then laundered to an unknown German who took credit for writing it. It was produced by a German who was a devoted Communist who had previously sought asylum in the Soviet Union. In other words, this play only existed due to KGB active measures, and it met with tremendous success too, as the play created a worldwide sensation. People around the world said the Pope was a Nazi. Nowadays, no one has heard of "The Deputy," but its resulting anti-Catholic animus still permeates our world.

American culture has been rotting for a long time because of this communist subversion. That's just a fact. I'm not stating opinions or telling you what to think. I'm saying go look it up, go study this. You've got to know this history, because otherwise, you're going to live with false history. False history is what destroys people.

13. YOUR MOM LIED TO YOU

Disney has been lying to us. Our Moms have been lying to

us. Our whole culture has been lying to us. They took the real nature of relationships between men and women and flipped it upside down. When we see this, and understand the true nature of relationships between men and women, it can hurt. It's tough to realize that we were blue-pilled.

A lot of people will resist Red Pill ideas because they're uncomfortable and painful. It's much easier to put your head in the sand than to deal with the uncomfortable feeling of having an alarm clock go off in your soul. The term Red Pill comes from the movie, *The Matrix*, when the main character Neo took a red pill to wake up. You know how people wake up? An alarm clock. Nobody likes to hear that.

If you resist that momentary pain, then you won't be able to see the truth. But you've got to understand these intersexual dynamics. It's important to learn about them along with the family, Communism, atheism, and religion. It's all connected. Being red-pilled means that you recognize the backwards nature of where the world is going now. The world is going in a really bad direction.

It's a hard conversation to have without being judged, because most people cannot handle that alarm clock. But I know I'm called on to be an alarm clock. That's my job. I'm here to be an alarm clock and smack the hell out of you to wake you up.

14. BOOKS ON FAPPING

Another level to learning is vocational reading. Don't take your job lightly.

I remember an email I got years ago. It said, "Elliott, what do you think about the Red Pill?" At the time, I knew nothing about the Red Pill. He ended up sending me some reading material. Then, as fate would have it, a few days later a friend of mine also sent me a copy of *The Rational Male*. That's a great book on the Red Pill, and I read all types of related articles and books, and it really changed the way I think.

I'm so grateful to all the guys who have worked with me in my programs, like King Initiation, for introducing me to Red Pill ideas. It has made me a better husband, a better father, and a better man. I got red-pilled on the problems that guys are suffering from, but I didn't just get books on the Red Pill, I also got books on feminism, pornography and how it ruins your brain, and I even got books on fapping and watched the no-fap videos. It's all so I can do my job in the best way possible. It's my calling to serve young men, and I need to know it all. I need to do my job in the best way possible.

If you're not sure what your calling is yet, look at what's in front of you. Get great at that by studying. Even if you're into video games, then read all the blogs, watch all the videos, and study all the books on video games that you can find, and become the smartest and greatest gamer out there.

Dig into your vocation. Dig into your calling.

Reading is the gym for the mind; it flexes the muscles of concentration and broadens the horizons of thought.

STOP

Stop getting caught up in global news. In fact, stop worrying about what's happening even a few states over. It's so easy to get caught up in the news, but the reality is, most of it doesn't affect us. Worrying about it does us more harm than good.

Take this as an example. Let's say there's a hurricane—and we get big ones down here in Florida—well, it could be a real problem. But the truth is that if that storm is just a couple states over, not to be cold-hearted or anything, but it won't actually affect me. All weather is local.

It's the same way with news. It's so easy to just scroll and scroll through trending stories. But when we pay attention, and we're really honest with ourselves, it really doesn't affect us.

It's crazy, because if you pay attention to the news, you realize that half of the stuff they tell us is a lie. So not only do the flashing headlines not affect us, but even worse, they're just lies. The media is trying to stir up discontent, make us angry, and get us to react. They're trying to destabilize the family and break down men.

Keep your boots on the ground right where you are. Keep your morale high. Keep your focus strong. Whatever is going on a few states over, whether it's riots or some dumb government action, you don't need to lose focus and fall off the path because of it.

They're trying to ruin our peace of mind and we have got to be vigilant against it. It's important to be vigilant, to hold a stable mindset, without letting ourselves get carried away by the demons. They're out there, these demons, both literal and figurative. It's these various stimuli that affect our thoughts and feelings, causing us to make poor decisions and take actions that damage ourselves. We create problems in our own life where there really is no problem.

We see outrage porn in the news and want to react. It happens to all of us. But it doesn't serve us well because all weather is local. Don't let it affect you, and especially don't let it seep into your mind or seep into your heart. Don't let it mess with your physiology and make your breathing shallow, destroy your mind, and destroy your body, especially when their lies aren't even imminent.

Shun the evil press and stop paying attention to the gossip of the hour.

15. ADDICTION TO PLEASURE

Effeminacy is one of the root problems we deal with as men.

Let's clarify a couple of terms to start out, because a lot of people get it confused. Effeminacy does not mean feminine. It's good when a woman is feminine. When a man is effeminate, that's the problem. Effeminacy is the taking of pleasure in the constant distraction of thoughts, problems, and opportunities. There is an unwillingness to let go of distractions, or even an addiction to being distracted, that characterizes it.

This is a timeless issue that men have struggled with going back a long way through time and history. A thinker as great as Saint Thomas Aquinas, one of the most important men of the Middle Ages, honed in on this issue:

> For a man to be ready to forsake a good on account of difficulties which he cannot endure... This is what we understand by effeminacy, because a thing is said to be 'soft' if it readily yields to the touch.

In other words, effeminacy is an aversion to austerity, a refusal to accept challenges, and it carries a concurrent unwillingness to give up pleasures. When you think about it, these are some of the defining character traits of modern man. It's interesting that Aquinas was writing about this so many hundreds of years ago with such accuracy. Surely, the problem has gotten worse since then.

If we stop and take notice, we realize how distractions cause havoc in our lives. We not only have to deal with an abundance of sensations, entertainments, thoughts, and demands, but also the pleasure we take in those diversions. Then there is the tendency to want more of it.

We know social media does this. It exacerbates the problem, causing an increase in anxiety, depression, and dissociation from the real world. Social media is not the real world. Yet, it can feel so pleasing. It's so pleasing to get on Instagram and just scroll through, double tapping, and wallowing in the pleasure of all the stimuli.

What would the opposite of effeminacy be? Aquinas

explains that it is perseverance: "[When a] man does not forsake a good on account of long endurance of difficulties and toils." That means staying unaffected and unmoved by all the amazing and crazy things that try to unseat us. That is stoicism and masculinity.

EXTRA	STOP Using Your Smartphone! MakeMenStrongAgain.com/BONUS

16. BATTLE AGAINST YOUR DEMONS

We sometimes face the risk of getting trapped into our fallen nature as men. That's what we don't want to happen. Since the age of psychology began, people have addressed this problem by using all sorts of fancy medical terminology, so when a man is fallen, he is described as having: sadomasochism, narcissism, dissociative identity disorder, or something similar. This approach is supposed to help men, but really, the results have not been great, and there are more fallen men than ever. The problem is that when you see a problem as a psychological pathology, it implies that it's yours, and now you own it.

Men used to think and talk about this problem very differently, and while it may sound archaic to our ears, when a man became trapped in his fallen nature, they blamed demons. Let's talk about these demons, because this is actually a very resourceful and useful way to think about it. When we understand that we are up against evil spirits, as entities that hate us and want to destroy us, then we can pick up our sword and go to battle against the demons.

To me, that is a much more resourceful way of approaching this. Rather than thinking, "I've got a problem and I need a pill; I've got a problem and I need to speak to somebody about it; I've got a problem and I need it diagnosed." Nope. You aren't the problem. You're being attacked by demons. It gives me so much more strength when I recognize it this way.

These demons are seeking to destroy us. But they are not us. So if you are depressed, that's not you and it's not your depression. It's evil spirits seeking to destroy you. They try to disrupt your thoughts, your feelings, and your body. There's no way to be still if demons are attacking you.

That's why we name the demons. Then we can take action against them.

17. LEARN FROM THE CHURCH FATHERS

It shocked me when I started reading classic Christian writings. They were amazing, but no one ever seemed to talk about them, and I hadn't even known that they existed. Why would the Church hide them from us?

I wanted to know how monks found peace. These are men who dedicated their lives to finding stillness. They're not Zen Buddhists because they didn't pull from Buddhist scripture. These were Zen Christians. That led me to discover Ignatius Brianchaninov, a great nineteenth-century bishop, who dedicated his life to finding stillness through the Orthodox Church. The monks called it "deification": to live your life with the stamp of God.

By the way, my middle name is Ignatius. I discovered Ignatius' work and fell in love with it, and it turned out he had the same name as me, so that was quite a sign for me. I put the name "Elliott Ignatius" on my Instagram page to acknowledge my roots.

Anyway, he's one of the Eastern Orthodox Fathers. That's another thing that red-pilled the crap out of me. I'm sorry, but these days, most of Christianity is blue pill. But when I started to recognize that these men were called Fathers, that this is where patriarchy comes from, it really red-pilled me.

His book, *The Arena*, was a kind of handbook for monks. He wrote it for men who dedicate their lives to asceticism, fasting, prayer, and stillness. He practiced and advocated something like a form of meditation, but it was a more masculine form of meditation.

It's interesting to see that Red Pill and related ideas, which may seem new and modern, really have a deep history in our civilization. For example, Ignatius explained the need to stop wasting so much energy on women:

> As far as possible, avoid conversations with women, good man. If you're obliged to have dealings with women, keep your eyes cast down and teach those with whom you speak to look chastely... The figures of women, their glances, their voices, their tenderness and sweetness, make a very strong impression on our souls by the action of nature, especially when Satan cooperates with nature.

The Christian Fathers knew and understood many of the problems that young men face, and offered counsel. Of course, nowadays, society will deride and insult any man who puts aside women to focus on himself, his peace of mind, and his quest. Modern society hates and fears traditional masculinity. That's why we return to the past, to learn from the Church Fathers.

18. ENTER MONK MODE

Avoid the opposite sex. That's just my opinion, but it really is a good way for men to live, and especially young men. Instead of chasing tail and letting girls confuse, tempt, and throw guys off track, which is such a freaking waste, they can get real work done.

Monks didn't take a vow of celibacy for no reason. They knew it would help them to not get distracted and thrown off course by women. If you read Ignatius' book, you'll see he actually has an entire chapter titled, "On Avoiding Acquaintance with the Opposite Sex." He explained that the holy fathers "carefully guarded themselves" from women, not allowing women into men's monasteries, so that they could live attentive lives.

This advice runs contrary to everything that we're told to do and believe today. Well, the monks weren't interested in being politically correct. They were more interested in attaining peace and allowing themselves simply to be. They made it very clear: Do not be around women. That's especially true for a man striving to live an attentive life.

Women will throw you off track.

The feminists want to water down what is masculine. How do they do that? They distract boys with girls. Everyone used to know this basic truth and it used to be that men had space to be with other men. Even just a century ago, for instance, segregation of boys and girls in school was normal, and they had good reason for doing so. Well, that hardly exists anymore. So modern man is addicted to girls, addicted to sex, and addicted to porn. It makes it difficult to be virtuous.

That's why I like to say that you should go monk or marriage. This isn't to say you must take a vow of celibacy. Monk mode is great, but it doesn't mean you're going to be a monk your whole life.

EXTRA	3 Keys To MONK-MODE Mastery (2.5hr Presentation) MakeMenStrongAgain.com/BONUS

19. THE FIRE OF LUST

This one is a little crazy—I would not have been writing it even just a few years ago—but it's true. A woman will use her body to entice you with lust onto a path of destruction.

Many people will steadfastly refuse to admit this to themselves. They confuse masculinity with gawking at girls in Hooters and chasing that hot girl on Instagram. Traditional masculinity is different. Monks warned about women and even warned that involvement with women could be worse than a "terrible shipwreck." Here is Ignatius quoting the words of Saint Macarius the Great, who lived back in the fourth century:

> The heat of a lighted lamp melts butter, and the fire of lust is stirred up by the company of women. A woman's face is a cruel dart that inflicts a wound in the soul. If you wish to be pure, avoid the Society of Women like poison, because in their society there's a strong pull of sin, like the pull of ravenous beasts. It is not so dangerous to be near a fire as to be near a young woman. Avoid while you are young, the turbulent action of impure passion and the society of women. Those who fill their stomach and at the same time hope to acquire purity are deceiving themselves. More terrible is the shipwreck from the look of a beautiful face than shipwreck from a storm at sea. The face of a woman if formed in the mind will force one to neglect the very custody of the heart. Flame placed in straw will produce a fire; so impure passionate desires flare up from dallying with the remembrance of a woman.

It sounds crazy, and this is a tough pill to swallow, but I'm just putting this out there for you to consider. It's one of our pillars of traditional masculinity: *Stop*. Eating too much? *Stop*. Using porn? *Stop*. Chasing women? *Stop*.

Stopping will produce calmness in body and mind. Nothing against women, but if you are striving to have some control over your life, then this is a good warning to keep in mind. Let's move on here and look at this next passage:

> It should be noted that a woman who has become

acquainted for quite a short time with a monk living in a well-ordered monastery or receiving instruction from a spiritual elder considers it her first duty to draw her lover out of such a monastery and draw him away from his elder or spiritual father in spite of the obvious benefit to the monk of the strictness of the monastery and the instructions of the elder. She wants to have exclusive possession of the object of her passions. In her madness, she regards herself as sufficient and able to take the place of the elder whom she considers and declares to be most inadequate and incapable. She will spare no means to attain her ends—neither means supplied by the world, nor means provided by Satan.

I even see some of this with my wife. I have to shut her out sometimes when I want to pray, when I want to meditate, or when I just want to be. The fact is that women are jealous and they can even be jealous of our relationship with God. You see this play out in the story of the Garden of Eden. Adam was in a perfect relationship with his Father, and Eve was the one who was dissatisfied with that arrangement, and she wanted to be the focus of Adam's attention.

Sometimes a man has to go off to battle. He's going off to do something manly: maybe he's going to meditate, or maybe he's going to fight. But that's not what the woman wants and she may try to obstruct the man. That's why the monks advised to stay away from women. Sometimes, you've got to stay away.

20. DON'T ARGUE WITH THE DEMON

The demon wants you to overthink. He wants you to be anxious, depressed, worried, and afraid.

Ignatius wrote:

> The way for a beginner to struggle with an invisible spirit that is visible only to the mind in thoughts and visions is to reject the sinful thought or vision immediately without entering into conversation or argument with it, so that the thought or fantasy may not have time to make any impression on the mind and so get possession of the mind.

That means don't even argue with it. Don't converse with it. Don't pay any attention to it.

I've seen that Ignatius is right. When I'm falling into a problem and I feel the demons attacking me, if I stop to consider and judge my thoughts, it only lets the demons attack me more.

So I say, don't judge yourself; stop judging yourself. That's demonic. The demons want you to get caught up with thoughts like, *Oh, I should have more of this. I should have done that. Why don't I do this?* But all of that is pure demons trying to destroy you.

Saint Isaac the Syrian of the seventh century offers some great advice to cut off arguments with evil:

> Not to contradict or argue with the thoughts cunningly sown in us by the enemy, but to cut off all intercourse with them by prayer, is a sign of a mind that has found

wisdom and power by grace. Its true understanding of the situation frees it from much (vain and superfluous) labor... we do not at all times have the power to reduce to silence all opposing thoughts by argument and to conquer them. For the most part, we receive wounds[.]

The only way to win this fight is to not get caught up with it in the first place. It's a trap. Stop debating your demons.

21. ASK FOR HELP

It's tough: the negative thoughts, the temptations, the demons.

If you can't beat them relying only on your own will, then ask for help. God wants to help you. God wants to see you victorious. God doesn't want the demons to win. He'll allow the demons to test you to help build your strength, just like any good coach, but he wants you to win, just like your coach wants you to win. So he gives you the tools and says, "Seek my guidance, my support, and my strength."

Here is one final passage from Ignatius, recommending prayer as a reliable weapon to stop negative thoughts:

But when the passions are roused, and the mind is darkened and confused at the enormity of the temptation, and thoughts assail with persistence and fury, then—not only against lustful thoughts, but also against thoughts of anger, sadness, despondency, sloth, despair, greed, in fact against all sinful thoughts—the surest and most reliable weapon is prayer with the body's participation in it. Once again, it is the Lord Himself Who has given us an example of this and enjoined it. In His agony before His death in the garden of Gethsemane, the Savior of the world, bowed His knees and fell on His face and prayed prostrate.

Beat the demons. Be vigilant.

22. **PRAY**

To help humble your heart, and give you strength in challenging times, here's a little prayer: *Lord Jesus Christ, have mercy on me.*

This is the Jesus Prayer. You can train yourself so that your first thought and action on waking from sleep is the Jesus Prayer. Try to train yourself with the Jesus Prayer to such an extent that it becomes an unceasing prayer.

Just breathe in and say, "Lord Jesus Christ, have mercy on me." This is my mantra, my meditation. It's where I go to seek peace, support, and stillness.

Use the Jesus Prayer, or if not, go ahead and create a mantra for yourself. Something like, "I'm whole, powerful, strong, harmonious, and happy." But for me, I like the Jesus Prayer. Breathe it in, breathe it out. Say the Jesus Prayer. Make it a part of your heart. Send the demons away. Clear the mind.

✗

Silencing the mind's ramble clears the path for God's voice.

FAST

People sometimes fast to lose weight—that's great and it works well—but I got into fasting for a different reason. Fasting is amazing for shutting down the ego. This is how you can cleanse your spirit.

When people talk about "spirituality," a lot of times we get unsure and confused, because it's not easy to calm down the ego. It puts some people off at first. But it's really not as mystical as it sounds. And the truth is that man can only get so far on pure materialism. He needs something higher in his life to be truly strong. It's a necessary part of traditional masculinity.

Our twelve pillars build towards calming the ego, and towards our final and greatest pillar, allowing ourselves simply to *be*. Learning to fast is a crucial part of this journey, because when you fast, you humble yourself. There's a battle to calm down your ego and force it to take a back seat. It brings about clarity in your life. Much of the excess that we had sought after will fall away. That's when the strongest version of yourself will rise to the surface.

23. I DIDN'T KNOW I HAD DEMONS

Years ago, I got into New Age fads, astrology, and even the occult. I hired psychics and started smoking weed. Basically,

I became a hippie.

It seemed to me, at the time, that I had to get in touch with my feminine side. If you saw my videos on YouTube back in the day, then you know what I'm talking about. I hired some mentors, you may know them, but I won't print their names here, who told me that I needed to get in touch with my feminine side. That's exactly what I did.

Let me tell you, it turned out poorly. My life began to break apart and I fell into a very dark place. But that was what the world was telling me to do, right? So I did it. And it's not just me that this has happened to. There are many guys out there who get trapped in this dark hole, this effeminate dungeon, this feminist cave. For some of them, they get stuck in there from the very time that they were children.

In my case, I now recognize that it was an attempt to run away from my fears and inner demons. That all came as a surprise to me because I didn't know that I had demons. Nobody had spoken to me in those terms. So, for me, the first step to getting free was simply recognizing the demons. At first, I resisted out of fear, and when God told me to fast, I just got deeper into my weed addiction. As long as I resisted, problems only kept getting worse. That went on until I finally humbled myself, listened, and began to fast. Today, I'm grateful for that whole experience, and even the dark times, because it's how I evolved into who I am.

Fasting is amazing. Because when you begin, you can create distance between yourself and your incessant thoughts. That's what I mean when I write about demons. Some people talk about literal demons with wings and fur. And maybe they can see that, who knows? But I'm talking about the incessant negative whispers in your head and heart coming from the enemy. When you fast, you force them to the surface, where you can recognize them, and ultimately overcome them.

By the way, just a warning, but there is such a thing as prideful fasting, which you need to watch out for. I know because I did it. But when you fast and allow yourself to go into the depths of humility, you begin to recognize just how frail you are. There's no way to fix a problem while it stays in the shadows, and there's no way to work on fragility until it's exposed. Fasting will expose your fragility. When you fast, all those frailties, inner beta tendencies, weaknesses, incessant negative thoughts, and demons, they come to the surface.

Then you will see the emotional cleaning process.

24. HOW TO GET CLARITY IN LIFE

Do a fast. You may not even have a clear goal you want to achieve, but just go ahead and do it. It's how you challenge your will. That's the most important part of this equation.

If we don't challenge our will, then we become weak. You may have all kinds of little, weird, and stupid addictions. You may be feeling emotional, depressed, and anxious. You want to get over these problems and find clarity in your life. That's a great time to challenge yourself with a fast.

If you've never fasted before, then start with just one day. Don't think about the second day. Don't think about the third day. Just get one day under your belt. That's my challenge to you. If you're intrigued by this concept, then tomorrow, don't eat. Wake up, skip breakfast, lunch, and dinner, then go to bed. See how you're doing when you wake up the following day. At that point, if you want to break your fast, go right ahead. You did what most Western consumers cannot do. Congratulate yourself.

25. SURVIVE THE ZOMBIE APOCALYPSE

Most Western consumers can't fast, and they're going to have a serious problem when the zombie apocalypse hits, and they have no choice. It's coming. It looks like there could be a total financial collapse, and then this whole Ponzi scheme will fall down. Another big risk is that the power grid could fail. It just takes one nuclear bomb detonated high above the United States to black out the entire country. That means supermarkets will close down, and fridges won't work, which means our food will spoil.

No matter what it is, whether it's a blackout, a financial collapse, or war with China and Russia, people are going to freak out. If they've never gone a single day in their life without eating a meal, they'll lose their minds. Most people don't know what it's like to fast, and they won't be able to survive, not because it'll be physically impossible to do so, but because they're going to freak out.

If shit hits the fan, the first thing I'll do is take my whole family down to one meal a day. If things get really bad, I know I can go three days a week, maybe Monday, Tuesday, and Wednesday, without eating. I won't freak out because I know I can do it.

Test the waters for yourself. See what you're capable of. That way, when the pressure is on, you know what you can do. Like they say in sports, you play the way you train. So train with fasting, because one day, the food trucks might stop. Maybe it will happen and maybe it won't. But you don't want to freak out like most people. It's not good to be like that. It's much better if you can be firm in your conviction that you have the ability to handle it.

26. AUTOPHAGY

Fasting also has tremendous physical benefits. It increases autophagy, which is the breakdown of nasty, old cells, which can turn cancerous. I'm not officially making this claim because I don't need the FDA coming to track me down. I'm just a meathead writing a book. But scientists have shown—and you can check this out yourself—that fasting can help heal cancer due to the increased autophagy.

27. FIVE POWERFUL WAYS FASTING HELPS YOUR BODY

BENEFITS

- Increase growth hormone
- Improve the immune system
- Less insulin
- Reset hormones
- Burn fat

28. BURN FAT NOT MUSCLES

You ever notice how so many women are on perennial diets that make them miserable, don't seem to work, and their health is iffy at best? It's because calorie restriction is one of the worst ways to lose weight. Fasting is the best. Let's get into the physiology here.

Calorie restriction just means consuming fewer calories than needed to maintain your current energy demands. Calorie restriction will make your body retain fat and burn muscle. With fewer calories, all sorts of bad changes happen in your body: it will lower its metabolic rate, mess with reproductive hormones and thyroid function, and promote muscle breakdown.

Unlike calorie restriction, fasting is a complete suspension of caloric consumption. Despite that, your body is still nourished and gets the energy it needs. Amazing.

Your body is designed in a brilliant way to preserve muscle. If you don't eat, your body wants to preserve the mechanism by which you obtain food, which is your muscles. It would make no sense if you don't eat and then your body starts to destroy the mechanism by which you go out and get more food. Your body thinks, *Uh oh, there's no food. We need these muscles to hunt and kill that antelope. Let's release growth hormone to maintain muscle mass while eating up body fat.*

In a fasted state, the body first uses stored energy within the liver. It may take a little bit of time before your body runs out of both energy from the last meal and energy in the liver. As long as there's still liver glycogen, you're still burning energy from your liver, and are not yet in a fasted state. Only after the energy from the liver has been depleted does the body starts to breakdown stored body fat for energy. That's fasting.

Fasting is a metabolic state. The two basic states are the fed state of anabolism and the fasted state of catabolism. For so long, they were attacking catabolism, at least, in the bodybuilding circles. I grew up reading bodybuilding magazines in the 1990s, and they said that you never want to be catabolic. But by demonizing catabolism, we lose one side of the coin. When your body is anabolic, it's in building mode. When it's catabolic, it's in breakdown mode. Both are needed and important.

The fasted state only occurs when all of the fuel has been used up and the body starts burning stored energy. That's why seventy-two-hour fasts are great. They make sure that you get into a true fasted state.

Sometimes, guys are hesitant to fast because they're afraid that they'll lose muscle. It may seem like that because you do use up glycogen, so the muscles will feel less puffy—when you're fasting, don't expect the pump. But that doesn't mean that you're losing muscle, it just means that you've lost the glycogen in your muscles. Your body will literally go ahead and produce hormones to maintain muscle.

It may be surprising but that is the science of what happens in your body. To keep muscle and burn fat, you don't want to be on calorie restriction, you want to be fasting.

29. STOP THE TRAFFIC IN YOUR BODY

The physical benefits of fasting go well beyond merely losing weight; it's great for general body health for all men, whether fat or not.

Here's a good metaphor that helps to explain the health benefits of fasting. Let's say you want to repair a road because it has potholes. You need to fix that road, but you can't because all these cars are zooming down the damn thing. So what do you do? First, stop the traffic. Only then can the repairmen get out there and fix those potholes. That's an idea used by Dr. Jason Fung, a smart guy who loves fasting.

Similarly, your body develops its own "potholes," diseases, and broken cells. But meanwhile, you eat constantly, so your body is always working to digest that food, all day, every day, for years. Sometimes, you just have to shut that road down, so your body can repair itself.

When you go ahead and give your body a chance to repair itself, a deep cellular cleansing process happens. A lot of people get triggered when you talk about "cleansing," and maybe for good reason because there are so many useless cleanses out there, but in this case it's true. And if you think about it, then you'll see that this idea of fasting isn't crazy or some New Age fad. For most of man's time on this planet, we've lived on the edge of famine, so fasting is actually a natural part of our existence. It's refrigerators and twenty snacks a day that are novelties.

Give your body a break so it can stay strong. It is incredibly rejuvenating to shut down the digestive process so your immune system can go to work on repairing your body.

30. RESPECT OUR ANCESTORS' WAY OF LIFE

The history of fasting shows that it was actually a widespread and normal practice. When we take into account this perspective, suddenly it looks like the people who aren't fasting are the ones acting in a weird way.

Before the modern era, the availability of food was unpredictable. Eating three meals a day, plus snacks on demand, was totally unheard of. No one had Costco food marts, convenience stores open 24 hours a day, or gigantic supermarkets.

Humans used to live with the seasons. We ate what was available, and naturally, there were seasons of plenty, and other seasons without food, i.e., feast or fast. We didn't have trucks bringing oranges from Florida to Canada in the middle of February. That's why societies often held periods of fasting right after winter: they stored up food for the winter, ate it all, then while they were planting for a new harvest, fasted.

Ancient civilizations eventually mastered agriculture and that reduced periods of famine. But all the great religions recognized the benefit of periodic fasting and voluntarily kept it going. It's a time-tested tradition. Jesus Christ, Buddha, and the Prophet Muhammad all share the common belief in the healing power of fasting. Buddhist monks are known to abstain from eating after noon while Greek Orthodox Christians fast for up to 200 days per year. Somehow people obsess over the Mediterranean diet while completely dismissing the fasting that goes on in their culture.

As a sign of just how important fasting used to be to Christians, consider this story. There's a moment in the Gospel where Jesus was brought a possessed man. Maybe the possessed man was just freaking out, or maybe he had epilepsy or some other neurological issue, but back then, they didn't know how to categorize it; I personally go back and forth between the modern medical definitions, and the ancient understanding of demons; I don't know which it was and I'm on board with both. Anyway, Jesus helped to cure that person. Then his disciples asked Him what happened and Jesus explained, "This kind can come out by nothing but prayer and fasting."

Fasting even goes back significantly before Jesus. Hippocrates was widely considered the father of modern medicine, and he prescribed fasting for obesity and other diseases of consumption. Diseases of consumption, I should underline, because that's what we're suffering from. One quote attributed to Hippocrates is, "To eat when you are sick is to feed your sickness." Greek historian Plutarch was reported to have said, "Instead of using medicine, rather, fast a day."

So there we have it, from ancient man to the Greeks to Jesus, everyone was fasting. The exception, the rarity, is our world. The modern religion is consumerism. It's just like the word sounds: consume, consume, consume. We never stop consuming. In America we are fat. We are fat as hell. And you know what they're looking for? The new diet. Because in America, we've got to consume. The consumer industry can't tell you it's okay to stop eating. People don't want to talk about simple fasting which would get to the core of the problem.

31. PHILOSOPHERS WEREN'T ALWAYS FRIGGING BOOKWORMS

Our superficial culture tries to box you in. Either you're a weak, scrawny intellectual, or a strong athlete who is stupid. But it doesn't have to be like that and people didn't use to live this way. Plato and Aristotle required students to train with the athletes. This was a time when philosophers weren't just frigging bookworms. These guys had to be in good shape. Guess what else they required of their students? That's right, fasting. Fasting is a physical and mental challenge that is a timeless pillar of masculinity. These were men who wanted to be strong in both body and mind.

Fasting is a potent remedy in a world drunk on consumption.

OPTIMIZE

There is a war on men. Our testosterone levels are being lowered with chemicals, pesticides, and plastics, in both our food and water. That's not arbitrary. A lot of people think it just kind of happened this way. But I'm convinced that it's not a mistake, and that it's being purposefully orchestrated. You can see that it's true because it's not just the chemicals—it's both chemicals and cultural.

Just look at what happened with President Trump. He reminded us of an earlier age when men were actually masculine. And what happened? Politicians, academics, and Hollywood all hated and attacked him. They want less testosterone, assertiveness, and aggression in the world. They want more emotion and more crying.

However, notwithstanding their massive attack on masculinity, Trump still won. How? Because deep down, people know that we still need these qualities. We need to make men strong again. Men need some level of aggression and confidence. Men need more testosterone.

A lot of people watch what I do on Instagram and YouTube and ask, "What happened to Elliott? When did he turn into a misogynist? How come he's so pro-masculinity!?" It's because I saw just how damaging the gynocentric female blue pill and white knight beta thinking is to men. The fact is that feminism does not work. "White knighting" does not work. It's that simple.

I have extreme opinions, so my pushback can't be light. We're not focusing on female virtues, like being nice, because it's not going to fix this problem. So I show up old-fashioned and overtly masculine, because that's what the world needs right now. People need a big masculine slap in the face. It's time to get that testosterone pumping.

32. THE UNPOPULAR TRUTH ABOUT ESTROGEN & TESTOSTERONE

If you talk about raising testosterone levels, people get triggered, and that doesn't just mean women, because even some guys will get upset. But there is an absurd level of hypocrisy here. Women say one thing about male hormones, but when it comes to women's hormones, it's another story altogether.

As soon as a girl becomes sixteen years old, boom, they put her right onto birth control pills. Some women even start birth control pills at the age of thirteen. That's just considered normal, standard behavior. Their families and society accept it, and even encourage it.

But birth control pills aren't normal. They use hormones to mess with women's cycles and support certain erratic behaviors. What do birth control pills do? They regulate hormones, or allegedly "optimize" them, and alter the level of estrogen in the body. They trick a woman's body into thinking it's pregnant. Why? So that she can be promiscuous. Messing with hormones is all fine and dandy as long as it's for girls so they can have sex.

The fact is that hormone optimization has been used for decades for feminism and promoting degeneracy and promiscuity. All of the "free" sex with birth control pills and abortion has done nothing good for the world. Nothing good. Just horrible things.

Then, after years of taking pills, when a woman's hormones are all screwed up, what do they do? They say, *Oh, you poor victim.* It's always about being a victim with some of these women. Then women get menopause and hot flashes, so they get right back on hormones. All of this in our gynocentric world.

But if you say anything about men using the hormone testosterone, watch out! People are going to get triggered as hell. People will accuse you of "cheating," like there is something dark about taking testosterone. Nobody questions birth control pills and estrogen for women. It's all great. But if it's testosterone for men, or even a medical application of testosterone, then people say, "Are you some kind of sissy?"

People don't want to speak the truth about how estrogen is promoted and testosterone demonized. Well, I'm talking about it.

You need to optimize your testosterone levels to be a man. That really means just living right. Maybe that means living extra-right since society is trying so hard to lower testosterone levels. But we're not doing anything crazy here.

This is about having normal testosterone levels, the way it's supposed to be, if you didn't live in a toxic world.

33. HOW TO MAKE YOUR HEART HEALTH STRONG

Why is testosterone important for your body? Let's go through the benefits.

First of all, testosterone will increase muscle mass while decreasing body fat. Guess what? God made men to have that naturally, not women, who have fat and no muscle mass. That's the way it's supposed to be. That's good, normal and natural. It keeps us polarized—sexual polarity. Men are supposed to have muscle mass. If you have a hard time building muscle and getting rid of body fat, then testosterone may be something to look into.

Second, testosterone supports heart health. It's funny because they put out some false studies claiming the opposite. This is a principle right here and one that we're starting to see clearly: If something is true, then the mainstream will you tell you it's false. It's so blatant that it's comical. But people are starting to wake up. Listen, if you want to know the truth, it's the opposite of whatever the mass media is telling you. Literally, if they say black, then you say white. If the masses are going left, then you go right. That's how you'll know that you're on the right path. So yeah, if they try to throw shade on testosterone, then you know you're on the right path.

Third, testosterone supports brain health. It improves mental clarity and can help with problems like anxiety and depression.

Fourth, testosterone prevents frailty. Men suffer from

mental, emotional, physical, and even spiritual fragility. But we are about being resilient. God made us to be tough and resilient, and that's what testosterone does.

Fifth, testosterone keeps inflammation lower.

Sixth, testosterone increases willpower. How many of us, how many times have we thought, *Man, I just don't have the strength to make this thing happen.* When your testosterone levels are high, your willpower goes up, and so does your ability to overcome challenges.

Seventh, testosterone improves sexual confidence. It increases sex drive and libido.

Eighth, testosterone helps you take risks. Maybe it has to do with my high testosterone levels, but I love taking risks. I'm a risk taker. Sometimes I look for danger just for the sake of it.

Ninth, testosterone helps you achieve a higher social status. The ability to take smart risks signals status. It's alpha male behavior. Testosterone makes you relentless, and it makes you a better leader.

34. **LEADERS, LEADERS, LEADERS**

Ultimately, the goal of this book is to help build up a strong class of men that can lead the next generation. My generation, Gen X, is screwed. Most guys I work with are millennials. Then there is also Gen Y and Gen Z. There's good reason why they're called Y and Z. It's because they're the last of it. It's the last of the degeneracy. The next phase is hard times. What do hard times create? Strong men.

It's my desire that you become an alpha male leader in your home, business, and with women. Leaders, leaders, leaders. We don't need more followers. The world is full of fake weak followers. Leaders, men. That's what we need right now. We are the remnant.

35. YOUR TESTOSTERONE LEVEL IS FALLING

Low testosterone is not just a problem for older men. Maybe it used to be that way. But nowadays a lot of 25-year-old men's testosterone levels are crashing and in the dumps.

Testosterone levels are dropping fast. One study found that the average level of male testosterone has been dropping one percent a year for decades. Some calculations show that the total drop in testosterone since the 1980s approaches a startling fifty percent. Sperm counts have also dropped by sixty percent. Think about that. Sperm counts have dropped by sixty percent. That's just straight-up crazy.

After I read up on testosterone and how testosterone levels are dropping, I got my own testosterone level tested. Mine is at around 780, and it was supposed to be between 600 and 900, so that was kind of nice. But on the other hand, I'm cautious, because the problem is who made that range up? Even our "normal" levels are skewed. Those numbers are kind of arbitrary and maybe it's really supposed to be 1000 and everyone's testosterone is so low that we have no idea. Then here I am, walking around at 780 and happy with myself when really a man with my DNA and my age should be at 1000.

There are things we can do to raise our testosterone levels. That's where optimizing our testosterone comes in. The first part is getting your testosterone level tested. That way, you know where you're at, and every six months, go and get another test just to make sure that you're on the right track. If it's going up, good. If it's going down, you've got to make some changes.

36. TESTOSTERONE DANGER

How do you know if you have a low testosterone level? Check out the symptoms below. No man wants to have these symptoms. It's why it's so important to pay attention to your testosterone levels and work to keep them high.

SYMPTOMS OF LOW TESTOSTERONE

- Anxiety
- Low libido
- Depression
- Lethargy
- Inability to lose fat
- Inability to gain muscle
- Erectile dysfunction
- Reduced cognitive function
- Indecision and hesitancy

37. REMOVE PLASTICS

Endocrine disruptors are everywhere now. They mess with our hormones and lower our testosterone. We need to be on guard against these disruptors to optimize our testosterone.

Water is a good thing to pay attention to because endocrine disruptors can get into the water you drink. There is something in plastic called bisphenol A or BPA and it's an "anti-androgen," which means it can block the action of testosterone in your body. When you drink out of a plastic water bottle, sometimes BPA from the plastic gets into the water. That is especially true if the bottle is re-used or kept in the heat. So consider not drinking out of plastic water bottles.

But with tap water, there's another problem. In America, most women use birth control pills, so when they piss, the estrogen from the pills end up in the sewers. Supposedly, that water gets treated, but unfortunately, the treatment systems do not remove estrogen from the water. So I'm living in this neighborhood and maybe on my block there's 400 women on birth control pills and that means 400 women pissing estrogen in the water that I'm drinking.

Get the best water filter you can. A good water filter, and drinking without plastic, can help your hormone system and body health.

38. NATURAL WAYS TO OPTIMIZE TESTOSTERONE

OPTIMIZE TESTOSTERONE

- Sleep
- No alcohol

- Sun
- Lifting

BONUS	Testosterone Boosting Sleep Secrets MakeMenStrongAgain.com/BONUS

Like a well-tuned instrument in the hands of a master, a man's optimized health and hormones play the symphony of his life's best performance.

DEFY

I was building a list of masculine virtues for one of our events: honor, loyalty, commitment, and discipline. All these amazing things. I kept nodding my head and thinking, *Yep, of course, masculine.* Then I read *defiance*. It kind of threw me back for a moment, and I realized, *Wow, yes, that's it. Defy* is a pillar of masculinity.

The problem is that modern society teaches guys to go along to get along. To be good boys. We are supposed to allow ourselves to be stepped on and walked over. We hear it all the time. We live in a world where walls are supposed to come down but not to be built up.

But this isn't how men are meant to live. Think about our evolutionary past. In ancient times, barbarians roamed about looking for towns to pillage and burn. As long as no one opposed those barbarians, there was just destruction. No civilization could grow. That's why men needed to put up walls. To defy the enemy. To create a special space on the inside where peace, nurturing, and growth can take place.

And by the way, that space on the inside is uniquely feminine. That's where women can exercise their unique prerogative to nurture children and the home. What could be more important for the future of our civilization than women fulfilling their divine purpose of caring for the home? It just shows how diabolically disoriented everything is that nowadays this responsibility can be looked down upon.

They work together. On the inside, we have women nurturing, and on the outside, we have men putting up walls. Defying is a uniquely masculine action.

39. IT'S OKAY TO BE THE VILLAIN

Nice Guy Syndrome is a real problem. It will leave you with no respect, no love, and no sex. Nice guys finish last. We can't be nice guys anymore. We have to be the bad guy.

There's this quote from *The Dark Knight* that stood out to me: "You either die a hero or you live long enough to see yourself become the villain." Batman never becomes an actual villain, yet he did live long enough to see other people accuse him of being one. I really feel that about myself these days. The guys I work with know that I work with a heart full of love, but it's a tough love, because that's what men need. They need mentors and elders, and I've put myself in that place, so I don't act like a nice guy. Some people watching from the outside may not understand. They'll say to me, "What happened to the nice guy Elliott? The fun guy who's smiling, where's that Elliott? What happened to that Elliott who we all came to love on YouTube?" Well, I had to become a villain because I didn't die the hero.

I hope you guys can pick up your swords before you die a hero. Chances are you're going to become a villain, like me. That's all right. We need more bad guys.

40. **THE WARRIOR CHILD**

Sometimes men have a hard time with *Defy* because of problems they went through in the past with their families. People don't talk about this much but it's important to consider. Here's a great passage from the book, *Iron John*, with thoughts on how childhood problems can harm and weaken us:

> When a boy grows up in a 'dysfunctional' family (perhaps there is no other kind of family), his interior warriors will be killed off early. Warriors, mythologically, lift their swords to defend the king. The king in a child stands for and stands up for the child's mood. But when we are children our mood gets easily overrun and swept over in the messed-up family by the more powerful, more dominant, more terrifying mood of the parent. We can say that when the warriors inside cannot protect our mood from being disintegrated, or defend our body from invasion, the warriors collapse, go into a trance, or die...
>
> If a grown-up moves to hit a child, or stuff food into the child's mouth, there is no defense—it happens. If the grown-up decides to shout, and penetrate the child's auditory boundaries by sheer violence, it happens. Most parents invade the child's territory whenever they wish, and the child, trying to maintain his mood by crying, is simply carried away, mood included.
>
> Each child lives deep inside his or her own psychic house, or soul castle, and the child deserves the right of sovereignty inside that house. Whenever a parent

ignores the child's sovereignty, and invades, the child feels not only anger, but shame. The child concludes that if it has no sovereignty, it must be worthless. Shame is the name we give to the sense that we are unworthy and inadequate as human beings...

Our warriors die. The child, so full of expectation of blessing whenever he or she is around an adult, stiffens with shock, and falls into the timeless fossilized confusion of shame.

Does that passage ring any bells? It goes pretty deep into where we missed the boat, and as an adult you've got to recognize this stuff. We need to recognize our naiveté, our shame, and how it manifests itself in a lack of boundaries, and an unwillingness to pick up our sword and shield.

The sword and the shield make a great image by the way, because those are the warrior's two main tools. The shield represents your no. It's the most important part of the warrior's equipment, because if a warrior cannot protect himself then he can't even venture out. If you can't put up a shield, then the sword is of no value because you'll be penetrated before you can do any kind of penetration yourself.

Use your shield.

41. BECOME INTOLERANT

A man without boundaries is no man at all.

There's this photo I saw, which is interesting to consider here. It had a woman with her finger pointing into a man's face and the man had his hands up defensively. It's a situation that's common that people just shrug off. But if you think about it, there's a real problem here. She is penetrating him with her body language. She's got her finger up in his face like a sword or a penis. The man has his hands together with a little opening ready to receive it. His hands represent a vagina. He is holding himself open for her to penetrate him.

It's degenerate: a breakdown and reversal of gender roles. This is the day we live in, where this sort of thing is accepted, and men who try to stop it, or merely notice it, are demonized as toxic.

But that's changing now. We're going to learn how to say "no." That woman, when she starts pointing her finger in his face, is trying to break down his inner sense of strength. If he lets her, he may not be able to get his inner warrior back. What he really needs to do is to open up his chest and say, "I will not tolerate that kind of language. You will not talk to me like that. If you continue, you're out of here; you're a dime a dozen, I can get another one of you."

Do not tolerate everything.

42. SAY NO.

Here is one of our most important weapons: *No*. It's true for every man, and it's especially true for men who have had their inner warriors swept away and carry a feeling of shame. I invite you to begin practicing. It's nothing huge, but practice saying no.

"Hey, buddy. Want to go out this weekend?" **No.**

"Hey, can I cut in front of you in line? I just have this one thing I need to get." **No.**

It's not about being hard-hearted or mean. It's about practicing your boundaries. Too often we default to saying "yes." I know because I've done it. I've been right there with you. How many times do we just say, "Yes," and go along to get along, but really, on the inside, we're cringing and thinking, "I'd rather not"?

A man learns how to say no really quickly when he has children. Sometimes my kids will ask for something and I'll simply say, "No." But then they come back with "But how come?" Children do that because they like to test you. Your friends and colleagues will do the same thing. They will try to soften and manipulate you to get you to change your mind. It all gets back to that sense of shame. If you hold a sense of shame on the inside, then you may waver and feel weak.

Well, say no anyway. I know it's tough, but it will get easier. You really don't owe anybody an explanation either. When you say no, it's because you don't want to. And that's it.

How do you get back your no? You start saying no. Just try it. Flat out: *No. No way. Nope.*

EXTRA	**Learn how to Say NO!** MakeMenStrongAgain.com/BONUS

*A man's defiance is his sword and shield,
upholding truth and righteousness in a fallen world.*

DEVOTE

Devotion is powerful because it's spiritual. It's a connection to a higher cause, something that is more important than ourselves. When we add that element to our lives, we also get a true warrior quality that goes along with it. Being a warrior is about having discipline and taking action, sure, but it goes deeper than that. It's about taking action for a just cause. It's about more than merely wanting to get something done. It's a willingness to do anything, even lay down your life, for your cause. There is no achieving in life, no beating the enemy, no slaying the dragon, if there is no devotion.

43. THE KING'S CROWN

The king wears a crown on his head. That crown is always there when we imagine a king in our mind. It's important for a couple reasons. First, it demonstrates his earthly power. Second, it has a deeper symbolic meaning, and shows his connection and devotion to something above him. You can see this because the crown is above his head, and it rises upwards, towards the heavens.

It's no coincidence that halos are so similar to crowns. They appear over the heads of important and holy men who live for more than just themselves. It's a glowing halo of light right above their head which rises upward and radiates out.

Make no mistake about this: Everyone is devoted to something. To eliminate devotion would mean a person is essentially saying they won't get out of bed in the morning because they have nothing to devote themselves to. So the important point to look at is what exactly a person is devoted to. If it's towards a bad cause, then devotion is wrongly ordered, and someone is subjugating themselves towards what is lower. When it's rightly ordered, it's a connection to something higher.

What are you devoted to?

44. IT'S GOING TO FALL APART

I've heard so many horror stories. I'm a speaker at the 21 Convention, and man, I've met many guys who spend twenty years devoting themselves to their family, then all of a sudden their wife picks up and leaves. These men give their lives to their families and then it's gone.

We need to talk about it because family is our people. It's a woman who you choose to be yours, and the children that you create, your flesh and bone. But the truth is, all of that is dust, even your wife, even your children. They are falling apart in this fallen world.

It may sound nice, but devoting yourself to your family isn't going to work. It will eventually fall apart. I guarantee it. That's why we devote ourselves to something above us.

45. WHEN I QUIT

I used to devote myself to my feelings. Yep. I've been there too.

Back in 2014, I quit YouTube. I made up all sorts of rationalizations to justify it, but now I recognize that I was just acting effeminate. It came from a commitment to my feelings. There was no need for me to quit. At the time, God revealed to me that it's important for me to deliver my message through that format, so I knew exactly what I was supposed to do. But I flaked. It was unfortunate, but that's okay, because everything works out the way it's supposed to, and I'm grateful that I had to face my demons and slay my dragons. That was obviously needed.

This is why it's important to have a devotion to something that transcends yourself. It stops your emotions from waylaying you. It keeps you on the right path. Having a higher commitment is a warrior quality. For a warrior to be in his fullness, to be rightly ordered, he needs to be devoted to something bigger than himself, whether that's a king, a people, or God.

46. THE ULTIMATE CAUSE

A lot of men I work with are millennials, and I get you guys, because I'm kind of like an old millennial. The popular culture that is forced on us is ugly. You're disillusioned with the material world. Half of you guys are in college debt, and you can't even get a job. This world is not built for you guys.

So you're looking for a cause. It's sad to see, but a lot of people fall into this trap where they get involved in Antifa or BLM. That doesn't turn out well. They're creating crazy amounts of chaos because their cause is the wrong type of cause. It's an earthly cause. They're trying to use their personal will to force a utopia here on Earth. It's not going to work.

Let me share with you my thinking. If God is not a part of your cause, then your cause is for mammon. You're never going to find a cause greater than the cause of Our Lord, the Lord God. Our earthly causes need to subjugate themselves to the divine. Remember, it's about the higher.

When you are looking for purpose, looking for a mission, looking for something to be devoted to, my suggestion is: It must be the cause of God.

47. BEYOND REASON

When I played football, I was running full speed and headfirst into people. I had no regard whatsoever for myself. I'd bear the pain and destroy my body, with no personal benefit, just to support the cause.

That faith is something that was given to me. I don't know, maybe it's a gift, it's a powerful way to be. Sometimes in life you've got to be able to bear the unbearable, and to do that, your devotion has to go beyond reason. Faith is required.

Some men have resistance to this point. Anytime you talk about faith and devotion then people start getting real cynical. The problem is that they've been taught to value logic over and above faith. They've been trained to be that way. By holding on to that attitude, by obsessively relying on logic and their lower-thinking mind, they limit themselves.

Open yourself up to faith and the higher mind of the King.

48. YOU'RE GONNA HATE ME

I have to be honest. Sometimes, I know what is right for my family, but my effeminacy kicks in, and I allow my children to do certain things that are wrong. I just don't want to deal with the pettiness.

My devotion, in those instances, is disordered. I'm being more committed to their feelings than to what is right. What should happen, and what I do a lot of the time, is just face up to it even if it will be unpleasant. I just say, "Hey, you're gonna hate me. You're gonna be angry at me. You're gonna resist. But I don't care, because this is what's right." It's important to be strong enough to follow through with that transpersonal commitment.

It can even be a bit isolating to live this way. Most people live by their lower qualities. They follow their whims while seeking out the approval of others. By contrast, the warrior tries to do what is right. The warrior lives set off from much of society.

It has to be this way. It's important to be devoted to the lofty, the high, the eternal.

49. ACKNOWLEDGE AND ACCEPT THE FLAWS

Be faithful to your religion, company, and country, regardless of its flaws. That's true devotion and it's really important.

How many guys do you know who've worked on something, but then when they face a problem, rather than staying committed to exposing and fixing it, they run away? I know what that's like, because I've done it. I abandoned Christ because I saw flaws in people. In college, I let the fallenness of the people around me turn me away from the Lord. That was an effeminate move and now I can see it. That's why I'm giving you this message: Don't abandon your devotion.

Years later, God called me to repent and come home to the Catholic Church. And brother, the Catholic Church is so flawed. I see how the Pope is a communist. I see how the hierarchy has pedophiles and homosexuals. I get it. But God was asking me to do something. I gave myself over to it, because God asked me to, regardless of the flaws.

Here's the rule: You don't run away, but you don't accept the flaws, either. You work to make things better. "Whistleblower warriors" are the people who are committed to the cause regardless of the flaws. There are always going to be flaws in everything. Everything in this world is fallen and is going to be flawed. But rather than allowing the flaws to flourish, they speak up.

If you're Catholic, or even if you're not, check out Archbishop Vigano. He's calling out other bishops for being frauds, and they hate him. But he's committed to the Church and he's speaking up. It's amazing to see, because he talks like a man who understands what's going on. He's not going for the globalist scam that so much of the Church has fallen into.

Yes, the Church has fallen into apostasy. But that doesn't mean you abandon it. You don't just roll over and allow the flaws to go uncorrected. Instead, acknowledge the flaws, blow the whistle, and fight. That's the warrior way.

50. DON'T CUT AND RUN

A devoted man does not run. A warrior's faithfulness does not allow him to quit.

There was a time when I was thinking about joining the Marines, God bless their souls. At the time, I let my effeminacy get in the way, so I never ended up joining. But I watch them, and had been thinking for a long time, *Wow. I hate how they make everything politically correct. If I were in the military, it would just be straight up impossible.* But now, my understanding is different. I recognize that may just be a man's dharma. Sometimes a man has a responsibility towards something. Even if you hate it, even if you're not aligned with it, you still do it. It sounds crazy in a world where we're taught that rebellion is the right way. But the truth is that when you've devoted yourself to something, like the military, you take orders. It doesn't mean you can't be a whistleblower, it doesn't mean that you don't speak up, but at the same time, you don't run away. You try to do the best that you can, where you are, while you're in it.

Stay with it. Don't let the flaws of the leaders turn you away. When you make a commitment, stick with it, stick with it through faith. That's what's required. If you want to unleash your inner warrior, it's through devotion.

*True strength in a man is found in his devotion
to something greater than himself. It's a beacon,
guiding him beyond ego, towards noble purpose.
In this devotion, he finds his truest power.*

REVEAL

Guys often ask me what they should do with their lives. They want to send their warrior out, but they aren't sure what cause to get behind. The reason they're confused is that they aren't listening to what's being revealed to them. Here's the key question: What's right in front of you? That's where the revelation is going to be. If you want to know what to do, where to take action, just look at what's right in front of you. *Where can I put the next step?*

The problem is that often we get carried away by our imagination and feelings. It's another trap of our world. We're taught to believe and overvalue our thoughts. But feelings have nothing to do with the present. If we allow ourselves to be caught in our thoughts then we're existing in an imaginary world, and we never end up doing anything.

In fact, I'm going to go a step further: A lot of those distracting feelings and thoughts are demonic. Whether you believe in a spiritual realm or not, there is a constant barrage of demonic thoughts we're subjected to, from the news, music, social media, and more. When you combine man's fallen nature with the world itself, then dark matter can embed itself in our minds and hearts. It gives us perverted thoughts: greed, fear and anger. We can stray from our true path.

So when you're struggling with which step to take, just

simply stop and look at where your feet are. You can't take another step if you don't look at where you are and you're not honest about where you're going. Stop, look, and make the best decision based on what's right in front of you.

51. **THE SLAP OF GOD**

Sometimes we feel like we're off-kilter. We want to know what the next step is, but when we look around to figure out what's going on, we don't like what we see. Well, that right there is the revelation.

It may be that all of a sudden you wake up and are like, *Whoa, this is a pigsty, look at me, I'm forty pounds overweight, what on earth am I doing?* It may be scary and for that reason a lot of people don't accept what is shown to them. Instead they prefer to continue living in an illusion. You can see this clearly with alcoholics and drug addicts who have to hit absolute rock bottom before they are forced to make changes and accept the truth.

Here's the thing. Revelation isn't some event where the clouds open up and the beautiful sun shines down. If you wait for that you're going to be waiting a long time. These revelations aren't always something beautiful—sometimes they're ugly, but that's the revelation, that's what's being shown to you.

Accept that slap to your face from God so you can get back on the path.

52. WAITING FOR MOMMY TO TELL US

One form of effeminacy that shows up in men today is our inability to choose. That's a problem, because decisiveness is a masculine quality and not having it is a sad weakness for a man.

Why are we indecisive? Because we've been taught to distrust ourselves, and instead to put our faith in "experts." We're waiting for the teacher to tell us. We're waiting for our Mommy to tell us. We're waiting for our psychologist to tell us. In the presidential election, we waited for politicians to tell us what to do, just like during the Covid lockdowns, we waited for "scientists" to tell us what to do. Nobody uses their own brain to discern for himself. Everybody looks to everyone else for judgment about what they need to do with their lives.

But the best answers for you and your life won't come from those people.

53. LOOK FOR GOD'S PATTERN

We no longer trust in the Father—God the Father—to show us the way. Instead, people make the mistake of relying more on the mother, or material world. This causes disorder.

Let's take a close look at the word *father* to understand better what's going on here. It has the same root as the words *patriarchy* and *pattern*. What is a pattern? Well, a pattern is not the actual thing itself. For example, a blueprint of a building is not the building, it simply gives you insight as to what the building can be, and is the plan by which the building will be manifested. A pattern is a type of plan.

We don't acknowledge the pattern or the Father in our lives. Most of us forget that we're spiritual beings. Some don't even want to acknowledge that we have a spirit in the first place. We've been taught to focus on the other side: *mother, matter, material.* In our gynocentric world, which has become diabolically disoriented, we are subject to evil because of our dependence on the illusion of the material world.

That's not to say that the material world doesn't exist. But the pattern is what forms the matter. That's the bottom line. Think of it in terms of how you become what you are. Your father's seed inserts itself into the matter of your mother: pattern into matter. The DNA within the male sperm determines whether you're a man or a woman. That's very telling. It's the father who makes that decision. It's his X or Y chromosome which is going to manifest as either male or female.

The giants of history thought in terms of patterns from God. Leonardo da Vinci, one of the greatest men ever, worked this way. Da Vinci wasn't interested in recreating the material, physical image before him. He had the sense that if he could get into the mind of the Creator, and understand the pattern by which God brought forth life, then he could bring it forth through art. He created a revolution in art. Compared to the art that was typically done at the time, his artwork almost came to life. By looking at that pattern from

God he created art with a more life-like feel.

Everything in the material world—every single thing—is a manifestation of the pattern showing itself in matter.

54. **ALLOW IT TO UNFOLD**

Sometimes we don't know what to do. We carry an angst with us. Some people say that's because the answer hasn't been revealed yet, but that's not it, and nine times out of ten the answer is already there in front of us. The problem is that we just speed right by it.

We live in an atheistic world and are taught to not trust God. This makes it very hard for people to see meaning in anything that happens in our lives. Even when the answer is being revealed, maybe even in a divine or supernatural way, we're just not trusting enough to see it. That's why I enjoy this interesting way of looking at life in terms of allowing things to be revealed. Slow down and allow the decision to unfold itself.

55. **START WITH THE MAN IN THE MIRROR**

You've got to be honest with yourself. It's true that this can be hard sometimes, and especially so because in our society we've been led to feel guilty and ashamed, but every single man harbors some darkness, and there is no good option other than calling forth your sins. That's how you are able to repent and make use of them.

It helps to think about it in terms of a shadow. We sometimes want to turn away from our shadow and pretend that aspect of ourselves doesn't exist. *I'm not lustful*, but you are; *I'm not arrogant*, but you are; *I'm not deceitful*, but you are. All of those things are inside of you. People lie to themselves. But the first part of revealing anything is revealing who you are to yourself.

Here's one thing that's for sure: We project that shadow onto other people. We look at other people and instead of seeing them, we see our own shadow. Most of the time, we're projecting our own problems onto others.

You have to look in the mirror. Start with accepting it in yourself. If you see something out in the world that you don't like, well, I'm starting with the man in the mirror. I'm asking him to change his ways first. Starting with the man in the mirror, and that was a great song by Michael Jackson, wasn't it? That's where you've got to start.

No matter what it is that you see out in the world and are trying to change or want to conquer, you have to be honest with yourself first, you've got to see it in yourself.

Honesty is the armor of the soul; a man must wear it always.
In this unwavering honesty, he forges and reveals
his unbreakable character to himself and the world.

ACT

Men get stuck in a dark, low, and disgusting place, when being indecisive. Sometimes it happens because we're afraid to be wrong. But let me tell you, it's okay to make mistakes, and just because you do, doesn't mean that you took the wrong course. Here's an example. Remember how I quit YouTube years ago due to my effeminacy? It was disordered on my part and I understand that now. But here's the thing: It wasn't wrong. It taught me crucial life lessons. I can tell you right now that the only way I can write this book for you is because I made some mistakes. That's the only way I could be doing this with such confidence. I couldn't write to you with this type of confidence if I didn't first screw up.

It's really okay. Let yourself "be wrong," so that you can make a decision, and move forward.

56. DON'T LIGHT A CANDLE AND HIDE IT

You can work hard, hustle, grind, and build something great, but there will still be those who denigrate you. They'll try to slow you down and stop you, even in the great United States. It's almost like they have a communist attitude. That's just where our culture is at these days.

It's a problem, because from their disparagement, you can develop a sense of guilt and a fear of judgment, which will slow down your true work. I've been thinking about this a lot lately, because I have less time for letting obstacles slow me down, since I increased my goals in a big way. Life happens in seasons. There was a time when I was content, but that season has ended, and now it's time to level up.

You have potential, I have potential, we all have potential: Why wouldn't we fulfill it? In fact, it's almost sinful to live your life below the capacity that God gave you. God gave us various gifts and I can promise you He wasn't thinking, *Oh, I hope Elliott hides his gift in the basement.*

The Bible agrees with what I'm writing here. Jesus says: "No man, when he has lighted a candle, puts it in a secret place or under a basket, but on a candlestick, that they which come in may see the light." There's a certain light within you that must shine in order for you to fulfill your divine obligation on this planet and maximize all that God has given you. If you play less than your ability, when you come to your judgment, I think God is going to look at you like: *You wasted a lot of time, bro. There was a whole lot you could have created, people you could have helped, and greatness that could have flowed through you. But you blocked that. You got in the way because you were afraid of what people would say.*

Obsessing about what other people think is one of the greatest obstacles that will delay us in our lives. People are waiting for others to validate them. It's a sin. It's one of the things that blocks us from our blessings. It blocks us from opening up to the grace of God and allowing Him to work miracles through us.

Who can argue with a man who's maximizing his potential, making millions of dollars, and he's doing it all for the glory of God? Sure, you can keep yourself down low, but how much more useful can you be as a man, a signpost, a symbol, and a shining star for God, by being the best that you can be?

57. THE UGLY BONOBOS

There's a stupid book out there written by a bunch of "experts" in which these idiots say that humans are dumb, primitive, and must act like animals. Even worse, they choose the absolute worst animal for us to model ourselves after: the bonobo.

If we really have to choose between animals, then definitely choose the chimpanzee. Chimps are patriarchal, aggressive, and tough. The bonobos, on the other hand, well these dumb animals have a masturbation culture, a matriarchal culture, a culture where females rule and males jerk off. That's kind of where we're at right now. Men spend their time jerking off to porn and women push men around. It's sad how much modern society has adopted these bonobo behaviors.

If you listen to the "experts" about lowering and debasing our human nature, you're going to end up living like bonobos, which actually is right where we are. But you don't want to be a bonobo. You want to be a benevolent, noble being. You were created noble.

58. DON'T BE ACTIVE—TAKE ACTION

Let's break down the difference between activity and action. Because they're very different, but it's easy to confuse the two or even not realize there's a difference.

Activity comes from fear and neediness. When we're in this mental state, even when we work hard, we're just wasting energy. Action, on the other hand, comes from a place of peace. This is where you want to be. Note that if you judge what someone does based on superficial appearances, it can be hard to see the difference. The difference is in a man's intention and internal state.

I was active far too often as a byproduct of guilt. If I found myself with leisure time, then I felt lazy, and just had to do something. It took me a long time to realize that worthwhile action can't come out of angst and fear. Sure, it's great to have a sense of urgency, but when the urgency is based on fear, you can find yourself creating a lot of waste. When we are blinded by fear and stuck in activity, we often miss the very subtle hints about the opportunity right in front of us. I've spent a whole lot of time on wasteful activities by being hasty.

I remember that early in my career, I was afraid. Fear fueled a lot of my activity because I was broke, with bills to pay, and a growing family. Even if it was time to relax, well, I just couldn't be still. I was fearful. Sometimes, that emotion overtakes you and you're unaware of it. Later on, you end up looking back and realizing, *Man, I created more of a mess being stuck in fearful activity than if I would have just taken a nap.*

True action has to come from a pure place, a place of peace. Sit down, relax, and allow yourself to be moved. That's a hard thing to consider, but allow your path to be revealed to you.

Think about playing sports. Sometimes, you just get into the zone. It's the craziest thing when you're playing a sport and you feel like you're in the zone. You just feel calm, right? I like to think of Kobe Bryant, rest in peace, or a guy like Michael Jordan. These guys were masters of the sport. They got into these sprees, these three-point sprees, and wow, man—it's like nothing could stop them. They looked so fluid. Grace is the perfect way to describe it: they were graceful.

There's a sort of divine intervention when you're in this relaxed place. You let go and there's a fluidity in all of your action. It's an amazing thing. Who doesn't want to live that way? How amazing would it be to live every day with peace and calm, but still while taking deliberate action? Living like that, you just can't lose.

59. SIT DOWN AND RELAX

I took my son, Benjamin, to Idaho to do a father and son survival course. It was amazing. The instructor had so many great stories, but let me stay on track here and just share one, which shows the difference between action and activity.

He told us a story about a guy who was lost in the wilderness. The guy was visiting some family members, and decided, *Hey, I'm gonna walk through the woods*. It's a beautiful day when you take a walk in the woods. So he's walking in the woods, maybe an hour goes by, and he looks around and he's like, *Holy cow, I'm lost.* He panicked. Later, when his family realized that he was lost, they hired a tracker to find him. These guys have an intuitive sense, and develop a mastery, to sense your footsteps. They can go to the last place a person was and then track them through the woods using a process of concentric circles. So the tracker went there, and found the man's tracks, and followed them until he got to a point when all of a sudden, the tracker stopped, and he started shaking his head. He noted the spot where the man started freaking out. At that point, the footprints weren't just a normal walk, they were all over the place— there were steps going forward and then backwards, too. The tracker stopped at that moment. He had this strong sense of intention, or he just sensed the fear that was happening in the guy in that moment. The tracker continued to track him, and as he was walking he finally came upon the lost man. He was dead, lying by a tree. He must have dozed off and frozen to death. But the interesting thing that the tracker discovered was that right before the older man died, he had crossed a road.

What does that mean? Well, if you find a road when you're lost, then you know that you're found. You can just follow that road and it's going to get you back to civilization. But this man was so freaked out, moved by fear, and stuck in a mode of frantic activity, that he literally walked right past his saving grace. This is what happens when we get caught up in activity and are not relaxed.

There were two lessons that the teacher shared with us. He told us, "If you ever get lost"—and look, this is a metaphor for our lives—"whenever you're lost, the very first thing you have to do is stay calm. Relax. Don't start looking for useless tasks to do. Don't freak out. Stay relaxed." The next thing he told us to do was to sit down. He said, "Find a sitting spot. In that sit spot, begin to become one with nature. If you know you're lost, then you're lost. Don't freak out, because you may be lost for days, so instead begin to allow yourself to become one with the environment." Sit down in what he called a "sit spot." Now you can start to think rationally. Maybe the sun is starting to set, it's going to get cold, it's time to build shelter. What's around me? What resources are available? What are the animals doing right now? He told us to pay attention to the animals and maybe look at what they're eating. Where are they finding shelter?

Literally, when you find yourself in this last place, you stop. How crazy is that? Why would he tell us to do that? Because you begin to relax, and in that relaxation, calmness, and groundedness, you start thinking rationally. You start preparing appropriately. You're not washed over and disoriented by your own fear. That's the biggest difference. The biggest difference between action and activity is that you stop, you sit, and you allow for intuition and rationality.

60. TROLL GOAL TRAP

Some goals that we pursue don't actually belong to us. They

come from other people. These are called "troll goals." They can create great confusion because when we're chasing what other people want—when we're chasing these ego-driven goals—then our work is not aligned with ourselves and our truths.

Man, I've had to face some tough realizations looking at this. There have been many times when I felt tempted to make certain YouTube videos, but then later on I'll realized those videos would have been purely for my ego. So I try to listen to God when he tells me, "You're not ready yet. If it's supposed to come, it'll come in its own time."

This is where an honest self-assessment is important. What are a few of the troll goals you have mistakenly taken up? And after thinking through that question, ask yourself the other side: *God, what do you really want to create through me?*

That last question is the way I formulate it, and I think it's a good way to do it. If you're an atheist or whatever, you can ask it differently, perhaps: *What do I want?* But you may run into problems with that, because for the most part, if you don't believe in a God, then you are your own God. That question—*Elliott, what do you want?*—that's less important because that's more asking my ego and a lot of times that's not even what we're meant for. So you may just end up with more troll goals. Not judging here, but just saying that I find it much more resourceful to seek that wisdom outside of myself.

61. **SOUL GOAL METHOD**

Let's do an exercise to move past the troll goals and on to our real soul goals. Just a warning here, but going through this process, some things are going to be revealed to you that may make you uncomfortable, and this will humble your ego. That's just what happens when you finally face up to that one thing that you've been hiding from.

This method is inspired by the book *Writing Down Your Soul*. What does writing down your soul mean? It's essentially about shutting off your brain and letting the words and ideas flow out. It's taking off the filters, lowering your inhibitions, and being very honest with yourself by allowing the voice within to do the speaking. This is how to bypass the ego and get down to the true soul goals.

First, set aside a few days to fast. Fasts have tremendous benefits and they're going to be really useful here. Really, anytime you have something of great importance looming, it's a great idea to fast. All the great spiritual leaders in this world fasted—Jesus fasted for 40 days—and I'm just telling you to fast for three days. Your energy may get a bit low, but it's interesting because you may find that the lower your energy goes then the clearer your thinking gets.

When you are in your fast, then you are ready. Get a notebook and write fast, nonstop, for no less than two pages. Let it pour out. Let God speak through you. The way you get into that state is by asking a really good question, like, "God, what do you want to create through me?"

After you've written it, and divulged to yourself what

God revealed to you, go ahead and read it. Highlight the trigger phrases. Those are the parts of the essay that trigger you, the parts that you look at and think, *No way, I can't do that.* Or you look at it, and you're like, *Whoa, yeah, that's it.*

You're looking for an emotional response. Either there's going to be resistance or there's going to be a movement towards it. Both are equally important and need to be considered. If you see something and then you shrink away, then, you've really got to face that. On the other hand, if you look at it, and you're motivated, and you feel excited, well, there's a good chance there's something in there for you too.

Next, formulate your soul goal statement. Take those trigger phrases and decide how you're going to live your life to manifest them. You want to place your soul goal statement somewhere you can see it. I have it in a notebook because I read that notebook all the time. You may want to put it on the refrigerator, or maybe on the mirror. Then, in the morning, when you wake up and you're brushing your teeth, it will be there to remind you.

ACTION PLAN	**How to Reveal Your "Soul Goals" and Dominate Life** MakeMenStrongAgain.com/BONUS

Like a master archer who draws his bow in serene focus, true action emerges from tranquility, not the frantic dance of a troubled mind.

GUARD

Much of what at first seems pleasing to our ears and eyes will defile our minds. Think about scrolling through Instagram or TikTok. It may seem like fun and games at first, but all the while, they're projecting images and ideas into us, and honestly, there is even a spirit that they can transmit into us.

What does it mean to say posting on Instagram puts a spirit into you? Well, there's a spirit of pride when looking for likes and thumbs up: *Wow, look how smart I am for making this post, let's see how many people recognize my greatness with a like.* There can be a spirit of jealousy and envy when looking at other people's social media photos: *Why does he get that good-looking girl? Why does he have that car? Why does he have those abs?* There's also a spirit of sloth. You're scrolling through TikTok, and you're just being lazy. You can get something like couch-lock, where you actually get locked into the couch, just allowing your mind to be penetrated.

Some of the stuff you casually scroll through is damaging. Pornography is straight-up poison, and it immediately begins affecting your hormones and nervous system.

Then there's stuff that's just candy. That's what a lot of our entertainment scrolling is. And what is candy? Well, candy is sweet and it gives us a quick rush, but ultimately that rush dies off, and you feel sick. A little while later you get light-headed. If you're anything like me, insulin sensitive, and you eat too much sugar, next thing you know you're getting a headache. You're getting woozy. Then what do you need? You need more. You need another hit. Candy tempts you and makes you sick.

That is where *Guard* comes in. We have to guard against these damaging, yet sometimes subtle attacks on us. We have to be watchmen over the integrity of our minds.

62. WATCH OVER YOUR HOLY SOUL

We have to actively protect what's important to us, otherwise it will get destroyed. To illustrate this point, imagine a big, beautiful castle. It's not just chilling out there and people come in and out as they please. It always has walls, and those walls have watchmen on them. They're guarding it. That castle can only exist and be beautiful and important because it's constantly guarded.

So what exactly are the castle walls and watchmen guarding? They are guarding specific attributes of the castle that make it special. They're protecting its integrity, wholeness, wholesomeness, and holiness. Let's dig into these words here because this is an important point. Holiness in particular is provocative, and I like to throw it out there, because it brings the religious perspective out for us. In the West, we're so anti-God and anti-mythology, that many people cringe at words that represent the sacred. People will even cringe at the mere allusion to the sacred. But really, "holy" is an important word, and we need to guard over what is holy to us.

"Integrity" is interesting because people normally think about it in terms of a person acting virtuous and trustworthy. But you can also look at a more literal meaning of the word: the structural integrity of a building. If your castle isn't built well, and if its structural integrity isn't carefully watched over and guarded, then it can come crashing down; even the wind can knock it over.

Now that other word, "wholesomeness." I really like this word, too. We live in a world where everything is degenerate; that is, degenerating or breaking down. You know, this is going off on a little tangent here, but this all makes me get nostalgic and think about what living in America was like a long time ago. I went to Cooperstown, where they have the old Baseball Hall of Fame, and it felt like a throwback to an America that was wholesome—you know, fathers and sons in the backyard playing catch. Classic America, very wholesome. I grew up in the 1980s though, after the sexual revolution and in a decade of greed, so I see images of what life used to be like and feel wistful. I grew up in the same swamp that you're growing up in—though it's many times worse for a lot of you guys who have been growing up even later on.

Be the watchman over the sanctity of your mind. Think about yourself in these terms: integrity, wholeness, holiness. How whole are you? This is where being the watchman comes in. Guard your sight, guard the wholesomeness of your sight.

63. **VIOLENT SEXUAL REVOLUTION**

Women used to dress modestly. They wore long, beautiful, flowing dresses. Nowadays, things are different, and women walk around practically naked. It's really thrown in our faces.

When you walk down the street you see these women. They say they're free to do and wear whatever they want in the name of sexual liberation. But they aren't recognizing that they're being violent to the minds of men. So now we have to guard our eyes against seeing their half-naked bodies.

Girls in the gym really seem to enjoy doing this and distracting guys from their training. I remember one time when I was working in a gym. I must have been about twenty-two years old and living *la vida loca*. We're all told to do the same thing by Disney, TV, and the movies: Trust your dick; you only live once; let your base instincts guide your life. Anyway, there was this girl who was on the treadmill and she was dressed in an especially skimpy outfit. I remember this girl, and here was the problem: I could not take my eyes off of her. I walked away and had other things to do, but damn, she was very attractive, and I kept looking at her. She stayed in my mind. Man, she's still in my mind— I'm writing about her right now! There was a spirit of lust that was stimulated in me by the way this woman was dressed and the way she looked.

These days, my advice to young men is: Don't look. Just don't look. You see her coming—here she comes—and you know that now it's time to be vigilant. When I'm being vigilant, and a good-looking woman is coming, you know what happens? The watchman arrives. Boom! I turn my head away. I'm not going to open my soul up to the downward spiral of having her run around in my mind for the next two hours. Not even four minutes. I don't want to give her even a minute in my mind.

64. DISORIENTING INFORMATION

We can be gluttons for information. It really is possible to get too much. You risk getting your identity wrapped up in it. Furthermore, if someone is doing it for pleasure, then it can even become a form of effeminacy.

The fact is that nowadays, there is so much information out there, that it's disorienting, just straight-up confusing.

I used to have this problem. When I was in my twenties, I wanted to know everything. I was so curious. This was back when the internet first came out, before Google and YouTube. I was one of the first of my friends to get active online. I was studying, researching, going deep, and learning a whole lot of stuff.

Then in my thirties, I wanted to tell everybody everything. That's probably when most people saw me on YouTube. Looking back at those videos of myself, I can't even stand to watch them. I was an entertainer. I wanted to talk about everything that I learned. I was a total glutton for information and it became too disorienting.

It's just like food. If you're at a buffet, and you're slamming never-ending bowls of soup, or whatever, never-ending steak, you'll get to a certain point where you know if you have just one more bite of steak, you're going to feel sick. It's the same idea with allowing in, via our eyes and ears, too much information.

But now, I'm in my forties, and in a different place in life. I don't want to know about any of that useless and confusing crap. It gets limited and cut out. You must be on guard against what's going into your head.

65. WHY WE ARE CONFUSED

We seek worldly knowledge instead of spiritual knowledge.

66. GUARD AGAINST PROGRAMMING

Back when I was a teenager, I'd watch movies and then think that I was actually living in that movie. My reality got distorted. I watched gangster movies with guys from my neighborhood, that showed robbing, stealing, and drugs. Then, every single time, we went out and acted like that. So dumb and impressionable.

Don't think that you can escape being impressed upon when you watch movies and listen to music. Just look at television. Sure, most people don't even watch television anymore—not network broadcasting stuff anyway like when I was growing up—now people may watch Netflix and Hulu, but it's the same idea. Guess what they call it? Programming.

Remember back when the Covid lockdown descended

and sank its claws into us? There was a series on Netflix that everyone was watching: *Tiger King*. I was like, *Wow, they locked us up in our houses, and everybody just went to town devouring some stupid series on Netflix*. It's what some people's entire lives are about. They get together with their wives and friends and talk about it. They've watched these programs so much that they have inside jokes. They'll purposely try to remember lines from the series so that when they get together, they can repeat the lines. Just talking about it sounds like a bunch of morons with programming. They got programmed. I used to train people in the gym, so I saw and heard them have these conversations.

I want to slap these people. I was so proud not to know what they were talking about. I still am to this day. But when I go out for meetings or whatever, sometimes they'll get into some conversation about what everybody's watching. Meanwhile, I'm just thinking, *I don't know what the hell you guys are talking about*. I'm happy.

67. MY SIN

When people go wild about *Tiger King*, then I get prideful. I feel real good about myself for not knowing what they're talking about. It's one of my sins.

I can tell you another sin I have, too. I do get caught up in TV programming when it's the news. I'm not sure exactly why, but I sense that it comes from my fear. I have a fear of not being prepared for the future, that something big is imminent and looming. I eat that stuff up: Collapse is imminent. And it is, but I want to know, what's coming? When is it coming?

So I try to guard against it. I was successfully vigilant for a while and had stopped watching news right up until about April, 2020. Then I got hooked again. But 2020 made me start looking sideways at a lot of things in general, and now I seem to be clearing up again. My vigilance is firming up. I just stay away. I don't want it. I just don't want to know anymore. I'm tired of the news.

68. TWO BAD PERSONALITY TYPES

On the one hand, you have guys who are self-aggrandizing. They tell you how great they are. On the other hand, there are self-deprecating guys. They tear themselves down. You know what? They're both deplorable ways to act.

Someone who's self-aggrandizing has to constantly remind you about what he has accomplished. These are the guys who like to have one-uppers. I'm like that—it's my nature—but I've become vigilant and guard against it. I've mostly outgrown it, and don't need to prove anything or get into pissing contests. It's true that it's good to remind people of your accomplishments in marketing, because they have to learn who to like and trust. But to constantly have to prove yourself to others, well, it ultimately betrays a lack of self-worth.

Then there are people who are self-deprecating. It's really unattractive. A lot of men do it, and it turns women off. You can bet that their wives are just rolling their eyes.

These guys will do things like call their wives their better half, or say stuff like, "I'm so lucky that she's with me. So lucky that I get to be with this amazing woman." Get the hell out of here with that. That's not attractive. Women get their sense of power from the power within their man. Women want to be with the most powerful man. Men look for beauty in a woman, and women look for a man with power. If you keep deprecating yourself to her, she's going to start feeling embarrassed. She'll think, "I guess that means I didn't choose the most powerful man." She's going to eventually believe that.

It's a trash way to talk. Do not self-deprecate.

69. WOMEN ARE STOMPING ON OUR NECKS

Don't let anybody in our gynocentric world deprecate you in front of your woman.

People try it on me all the time, but I don't go for it. One time, my wife didn't come with me to an event we usually attended together, so this lady asked me, "Where's your better half?"

I knew she was only joking, but I don't let that slide. I looked at my left arm and said, "You mean this side with the tattoo? This is my better side. The other side is injured."

Don't let them pull that on you. Feminism is a cancer on this planet. Men, there is no need to subjugate yourselves beneath women. They already have big egos and they're stomping on our necks. Women are outpacing us in every

MAKE MEN STRONG AGAIN

realm, whether it's education, making money, or in family courts.

Why? Because men have allowed themselves to be deprecated. Men have bowed down. Well, stop it. We've got to stop it. It's not going to last long, either, by the way. When things start getting tough, the women aren't going to be the sword bearers. They're going to look for men—strong men.

EXTRA	**The Feminist Deception Revealed** MakeMenStrongAgain.com/BONUS

A man must guard his words, sights, and sounds with the vigilance of a sentinel. What enters his senses shapes his soul; let only truth and virtue cross the threshold.

CREATE

Men are designed to create. Men built civilization with hard work, suffering, and genius. A long time ago, men built the pyramids, and then we just kept right at it until we created the modern-day pyramids, our skyscrapers. We created huge cities, industry, technology, and religion. It was men who built all of these incredible things.

Not one of those things was created by women. That's not because women are oppressed, as many people claim. You can give opportunities to women for them to build, but they won't do it, because it's not in their nature. It's women's nature to procreate and create people. We can't do that. Men are actually trying to do that now, with weird cloning technology, but the fact is, we cannot create a genuine human being. We cannot help a soul incarnate through our body. We can't do it. There's nothing more mystical, magical, and amazing than a woman's capacity to do that. Women will work with what we give them and make it even better. We give a woman our seed, she turns it into a baby. I gave my wife a house, she made it into a home. A lot of great things. We work well together.

But if you look at the world around you, and really think about what makes it good for the life that women bring into it, it's all created by men. Feminists can argue all they want. They can be upset, whine, cry, shout and scream, but the bottom line is: Look out the window, everything you see was created by men. Men thought of it and then made it. Everything around you, from cars, to your home, to the road you drive on, to your computer, were thought up, designed, and built by men.

70. THE GENERATIVE PRINCIPLE

I love the word *generative*. It's related to the word *generation*. Think in terms of building for generations. Create something that outlasts you.

71. RIDE THE WAVE

Don't allow a lack of likes on social media to determine your sense of self. Guys, it's all fake. It really means nothing. This is coming from a guy with millions of subscribers and I'm telling you right now that those likes are meaningless. It's my career, and I don't even fool myself anymore. I used to trick myself into believing that I'm changing the world. I used to believe that. And I understand how people can come to believe it. But I'm not. The world is changing, and I might have something to say, but it's really God just doing what God does. I'm riding the wave.

72. CREATE WITH GOD

Our generation is godless. Since we're without god, we make up our own. That's just human nature.

The god of today, which people have made up, is oneself. The New Age is all about self-worship. But the problem is that you can't be truly creative with that mindset. Creating something of value is not a *taking* for ourselves, but a *giving* of ourselves. Being generative is about being generous to others.

Ultimately, when it comes to this process of creation, instead of making it about yourself, get out of the way. Let God do what God does.

73. RESISTANCE IS A CLEVER DEMON

Resistance tries to stop us from creating. *The War of Art* explains this idea. It's interesting how inside this book, Resistance gets personified and given a moral quality:

> Resistance is the most toxic force on the planet. It's the root of more unhappiness than poverty, disease, and erectile dysfunction. To yield to Resistance deforms our spirit. It stunts us and makes us less than we are and were born to be. If you believe in God (and I do) you must declare Resistance evil...

> Resistance is insidious. Resistance will tell you anything to keep you from your work. It will perjure, fabricate, falsify, seduce, bully, cajole.

Isn't that the truth? There have been plenty of times in my life when resistance got me. I fabricated excuses and didn't take personal responsibility. But I have to watch my language here, because remember what we were saying earlier about demons? Don't own it. It's better to point it out, objectify it as something external, and squash it that way. Basically, like the way it's done in the passage above.

Either way, this resistance, these demons, however you want to look at it, they're clever. The passage uses the word "insidious," and maybe that's right, but I like that word, "clever." They will make up all kinds of lies and do whatever it takes to get you. Don't believe them. Resistance is always lying.

74. LET RESISTANCE BE YOUR GUIDE

It's interesting that although resistance can hurt you, it can also be a friend. It's a guide.

The way I've seen and experienced this in my life is that you can know the right direction to go based on where the most resistance is coming from. Which is scarier? That's the way to go.

When men are struggling with a decision, I ask them, "Which choice is the scariest for you? Which one gives you the most resistance?" That's usually the direction you want to go in. It has the most potential energy.

Think about this. We use resistance to build up our bodies, right? We actually go looking for weights in the gym to resist us, so that we can grow strong. Well, it's the same idea with spiritual resistance. When you face spiritual resistance, instead of avoiding it, push back against it. Push against that spiritual resistance in your soul today, and then you can grow. Then, later on, when a spiritual problem comes up, a little bit heavier, you're going to be strong enough to handle it.

75. STAY STUPID

I love this one: Stay stupid. This is like tricking the trickster.

In terms of taking action in a particular direction, many of us, before we do anything, have to watch a hundred YouTube videos, read a bunch of books, and ask people what they think.

Don't indulge in that counterproductive behavior.

Look, I'm just going to do it like a baby. A baby doesn't research. You know that's how kids are even if you don't have children. When kids want to learn how to walk, they don't start by asking a bunch of questions, googling it, or looking to other people for validation. They're just committed to doing it. They are stupid in their efforts.

Don't trick yourself. Don't outfox yourself. Don't be so clever. Remember, resistance is insidious, resistance is clever. A lot of times, when you're trying to be clever, you're really just tricking yourself out of doing what you need to do.

I know that this works. When I was becoming popular on YouTube, pumping out all those "Yo, Elliot" videos, I was staying stupid. I didn't watch anybody else's YouTube videos. I didn't take any courses on how to do it. I didn't plan out what I was doing. In fact, I had no idea what I was doing. I asked nobody any questions. Not that there were a lot of people to ask back then, because YouTube was new, but I didn't go looking to copy what other people said was right. I realized there's a camera, I can say something to it, and upload it to the internet. Simple.

There's so much supposed competition, and people think they have to do what everybody else is doing. I remember there was some guy who started becoming popular with his hyper-edited videos. Then everybody started believing that they needed to make hyper-edited videos just like him to be successful on YouTube, but they forgot that he was a Hollywood editor who made movies for a living.

I personally didn't even do jump cuts. I didn't know that jump cuts were a thing. Somebody commented on one of my videos, *Hey, Elliott, it's a breath of fresh air to watch somebody speak without jump cuts.* I was like, *What the heck is a jump cut?* And then I looked around and I found out it's when they take out gaps in their conversations. When they mess up, then they cut it out. I mess up, and I just keep it rolling. Because why? Keep it stupid.

76. STAY STUBBORN

Staying stubborn means never taking no for an answer. Things may start looking bad, going sideways, and getting tough, but that's okay, just keep going. Do not stop.

For me, I know it's my nature to start something and come out of the gates like a bat out of hell. But after a while I'm like, *Okay, I'm done.* It's just my nature. It's what happened on YouTube where I came out hard, then boom, hit a wall.

But the stubborn person does not give up. He realizes

that resistance will try to fool him into giving up, and he keeps going despite everything. That's why it's helpful to use the word "stubborn" here. It's a strong word, almost even a negative word. Often, people will say "resilient," or "vigilant," to give the situation a positive spin. But being stubborn goes even further. Just keep bumping your head up against it.

I remember seeing how well this works when my daughter was a baby. Babies are frigging stubborn and won't stop. When she was learning to crawl she kept falling, hurting herself, and crying. It was crazy. She even lost her tooth a year or two before she was supposed to because she badly busted up her mouth. But she was stubborn and just kept at it. She kept crawling.

Babies are stupid and stubborn. That's why they evolve so quickly.

77. HOW WILL IT UNFOLD?

Blind faith is amazing. The fact is, that when you begin to create something, you don't need to know how it's going to unfold. A lot of the time, we're greedy to know everything, but that just ends with us deluding ourselves. We're just building a fantasy in our minds if we think that we can know what our creation is going to look like when we get there. When you start a creative process, you actually have no idea where the journey is going to take you. It's not your job to know the outcome, either. It's your job to have faith.

"Don't wait for inspiration. It comes while working." – Matisse

BE

Here is our last pillar of traditional masculinity: *Be*. I have a lot that I want to say with regard to it, but it really gets down to one basic idea that's really the main theme of this final pillar. We need to face our own mortality.

We cannot live—it's simply impossible to live right—in a world that denies, sanitizes, and throws out the fact that you're going to die. This is a fact: You are going to die. We're talking about becoming the strongest version of ourselves and becoming all God intended us to be. The important point to fulfilling your potential is recognizing that your death is inevitable, so you can properly organize your life and what is truly important in it.

78. YOU WILL HAVE A GOD

Here's an interesting thing about humans. You will have a god, and if you don't choose your god, then a god will be chosen for you. You will worship something. You could call yourself an atheist, but you're still going to be worshipping something: money, pleasure, women, or maybe something else.

79. **THE TRUMP GOD**

Look at how many people were obsessed with the outcome of the 2020 election and how many people worship Donald Trump. I like Donald Trump. I like his moves and I like his agenda. But Donald Trump is a fallen man, and maybe he is being guided by the hand of God, but he's not a god to be worshipped.

80. **YOU'VE BEEN SOLD A PAPER BOAT**

There's a paradox happening where we live fully for the gods of this world, but we ignore the God of eternity. It's such a strange way to live when you think about it. Life on this planet is short and what comes after is so much longer. Nonetheless, people have been convinced to focus on celebrities, money, technology, government, and more, and so they worship false idols and have a hyper-focus on the immediate present.

We've even made ourselves into gods. People worship themselves, maybe not literally, but if you step back and take a look at society, it's pretty clear. It's really what people do more so than anything else, because none of the invented idols have proved satisfying. Deep down, people know that they're all dust. So what do people do then? Turn in and say: *I'm gonna get mine. I want to only think about my feelings and do whatever I want.* It's freedom to be neurotic, do drugs, jerk off, eat junk, chase money, and live as a degenerate.

But you're going to die after this brief life. So you've

been sold a paper boat, given a false coin, and loaded with a bag of dust. Because all of this, every single bit of it, goes away. Why worship that which disintegrates?

81. SAVE YOUR SOUL

We become our best selves as men when we live close to death and mortality is on our minds. That's when our spirit wakes up.

But today, we live in a world where mortality has been carted right off and kept out of sight. When family get sick, there is no hospice in our homes, instead, we send them to the hospital to die. We don't even kill our own animals. We don't associate our food with mortality at all. Instead, we just go to the supermarket and buy meat.

But we don't properly live if awareness of death isn't kept front and center. The men of the past used to confront mortality on a daily basis. Because we live so lavishly, we forget that. And while we avoid it, men of the past would sometimes go out of their way to confront mortality. One of the things that brilliant men did, and I remember seeing several instances of this, is they kept a skull with them, a human skull, or a rendition of a skull. Why? To remind them that, *Memento mori, I could die in this moment.*

This is part of why I'm so attracted to Catholicism. They say it's hard to live as a Catholic, but easy to die as one. It's because we're constantly living our life with the understanding: *I'm going to die.*

It's important for men to consider our afterlife. It forces

us to set our current life in order. Part of the chaos we're going through as a culture is because we neglect this aspect so badly. We've been told there is no afterlife, that we're just a bag of dust and bones, that we're going to die and go into the ground, and nothing is going to happen. But that can't be true. That absolutely cannot be true. There's an energy that keeps us sustained. We have a soul, and a soul cannot die. A soul is consciousness, and all of your thoughts, all of your feelings—the guilt, anger, sadness, sins, and grace, that you've experienced—follow you after your death. They don't just evaporate. Your body disappears, but everything that you are on the inside, continues to live on.

So the question to ask yourself is: *How am I living this life? Do I deserve heaven in the next?* Live your life right. Unburden yourself now. For me, I want to die lightly, with just a little smile on my face.

82. CHOP WOOD & CARRY WATER

We've been fed this lie that life is about happiness and comfort. But it's really not. It's chop wood and carry water, then chop more wood and carry more water, then die. Life is about work and sanctity. Work your body and sanctify your soul. Chopping wood is for the body and carrying water is for the soul.

You've got to work. Maybe it's just around your home, but there is still plenty you can do, even if it's just to make life more livable in the little kingdom you have with your family. Create a garden, plant some trees, fix the fence, or get a pet. Get up and do something. Because when death comes knocking at your door, you don't want to be idle, caught up in your thoughts and feelings. You want to be caught working.

A couple decades ago, there was this professional strongman named Jesse Marunde. I was a big fan of his when I started competing in strongman events. Anyway, he died as a young man at the age of twenty-seven. You know how he died? He died during his workout. He was just doing a basic training session, and then he laid down—you know, I do it sometimes too, just lie down on the floor after a tough workout and relax—but he laid down and didn't wake up. That's how I want to die.

If you're worried about your family, then don't be. Your actions and character will be imprinted on them. When you die, do you want your wife and kids to think, *Oh, my poor Dad, my sad Dad, he died when he was depressed.* Or do you want them to say, *I admire my father. I'm proud of him. He was a strong man and worked until the day he died.* Which is a better legacy?

Legacy means a lot for men because men are spiritual by nature. A lot of people try to denigrate the idea because they're trapped in sensuality and obsessed with material comfort. That's a consequence of our effeminate world and the fact that women are more physical in general. They don't talk about legacy. That is, unless they're feminists, and in that case they have it all backwards, because no one remembers these women. But men? Everyone remembers what their father and grandfather did, whether it's good or bad.

Men are the spirit. In what spirit will you die: fear and trembling, or courage and strength?

83. SAVE THE WORLD

This idea will mess you up more than anything: *I need to save the world.* It's another lie. This world can't be saved. It's not meant for saving. This world is built from dust and will return to dust. Every civilization falls, the only difference this time is that it will be a global fall, because everything is so interconnected. It won't be like when Rome fell, or when Genghis Khan died. Those were big empires, but nothing like what we have today. This time it will be a global fall. But that's okay. That's what it's designed to do. So don't try to save this world. Save that which is eternal. Save your soul.

84. THE STORY OF RABBI ZUSHA

This is the story of Rabbi Zusha, a very short story, a classic story. It asks the question: Who are you allowing yourself to be?

> The great Rabbi Zusha was found agitated and crying as he lay on his deathbed. His students told him, "You lived a great life, Rabbi. You were kind, like Abraham, and almost as wise as Moses. God will judge you positively."
>
> Zusha replied, "I'm afraid, because when I go to heaven, God won't ask me why I wasn't more like Moses and Abraham. God will ask me, 'Zusha, why weren't you more like Rabbi Zusha?' And then what will I say?"

And Zusha was a great man too. It's not like he was a degenerate or a loser. He was well respected as their rabbi. So why was he distressed? Because as he lay on his deathbed, and looked back, he was afraid he had lived copying others, and hadn't been true to himself. God would see that and say to him, *Zusha, why weren't you more like Zusha?*

Don't be like what your Mama told you to be. Don't be like what I tell you to be. Don't try to abide by the fashions of this world. Be the way you need to be.

In facing death's certainty we can find the
courage to truly live; let it remind you
to cherish each breath as a gift.

AFP

GO FORTH MEN
AND BE THE
STRONGEST VERSION
OF YOURSELVES.

MASSIVE ACTION PLAN

Congratulations on finishing
Make Men Strong Again.

Your next goal, if you so choose,
will be to study the FULL in-depth
online **FREE** video course at:

MAKEMENSTRONGAGAIN.COM/12PILLARS

SPECIAL OFFER FOR MARRIED MEN

**Are You A Married Christian Businessman
Or Entrepreneur With Kids?**

Do you struggle with drinking, drugs,
over-eating or viewing pornography?

Your biggest roadblock to success in fitness,
business and family is a life-sucking vice.

**I Want To Help You Gain Total SELF MASTERY and Control Over
Any Bad Habit, Addiction, or Filthy Vice so you can be THE MAN
God called you to be, and THE KING your family deserves.**

If you're a high achieving man who knows how to take massive action,
but you're living a double life by hiding your filthy vice from friends,
family, co-workers or your wife, it's only a matter of time before it all
comes crashing down... but you can take action NOW.

$997 VALUE FOR FREE

Go to **MakeMenStrongAgain.com/Kings** to access
my KING TRANSFORMATION at <u>NO CHARGE</u>.

With my free 90-day course you'll expose the nasty patterns that
are silently ruling and running your life so you can destroy
them once and for all.

Making men strong again today starts with strong fathers.

Let's become the father's, husbands and Men of God that
were called to be... King transformation will show you how.

See you on the inside,
Elliott Hulse "The King Of Making Men Strong"

YOU SHOULD FOLLOW ME HERE

MOST ACTIVE

MakeMenStrongAgain.com

@YoElliott

@ElliottHulse

@ElliottHulse

ALSO ACTIVE

Classics

@StrengthCamp

@ElliottHulse

ElliottHulse.com

INDEX

A

Abraham, 122
Abrahamic religions, 15
Act (9th pillar), v, 85–95
    action and devotion, 67–68
    action comes from a place of
        peace, 88–89
    action vs. activity, 88–91
Adam and Eve, 32
addiction
    some are little, weird, or stupid,
        39
    to alcohol or drugs, 38, 78
    to distractions, 24–26
    to girls, sex, and porn, 30
    to knowledge, 14
afterlife, must be true, 119–120
aggression, masculine, necessary, 49
alarm clock for the soul, this book
    as, v, 20
alcohol, and testosterone, 57
alpha males, 6
    and leadership, 53–54
American culture, author's love of,
    17–18
Americans, fat as hell, 47
anabolism, 42
animals, observing, 91
ankle mobility, exercise for, 8
anti-androgen, 56
Antifa, 70
anxiety, 39
    and demons, 33
    and testosterone, 52, 55
    and wasteful activities, 88–89
    increased by social media, 25
apostasy, 73
Aquinas, Saint Thomas, iii
    quoted, 25–26
archery, true action as metaphorical,
    95
The Arena (Brianchaninov), 28
Aristotle, 47
asceticism, 28
atheism, 15–16, 20, 81, 92, 117
athleticism, ancient philosophers
    required, 47
Atlas Stones, i
austerity vs. effeminacy, 25
author. see also family, author's
    about the, vi–vii
autophagy, 41

B

babies
    are stupid and stubborn, 115
    author's, 115
    don't do research, 113
Bacon, Francis, 13
Baldwin, James, 16
barbells, 1
Baseball Hall of Fame, 99
Batman, 60
Be (12th pillar), v, 37, 117–123
Belize, 17
beta thinking, 39, 49
better half, wife as, 105
Bible, 11
    fundamental to Western
        Civilization, 15–16
    often misread and
        misrepresented, 15
BLM (Black Lives Matter), 70
Bly, Robert, quoted, 61–62
body language, example of, 63
bonobos, not a role model, 87
books
    can be judged by their covers, 5
    guarding against, 113
        even good ones, 14–15
    how to use this one, viii
bookworms, philosophers not
    always, 47
botany, 11
boundaries, setting, 61–64
BPA (bisphenol A), 56
brain health, and testosterone, 52
brain, attractiveness of flexing, 6

Brianchaninov, Ignatius, 27–28
    quoted, 29, 31, 33–34
    quotes Saint Macarius the
        Great, 31–32
Buddhism, 11, 16, 27, 46

C

calling, dig into your, 21
calorie restriction, 42–44
candles, not be hidden in baskets,
    85–87
candy, social media as, 97–98
castle to be defended, your mind as,
    98–99
catabolism, 43
Catholicism, vii, 15–16. see also
        Christianity
    hard to live as a Catholic, easy
        to die as one, 119–120
    shortcomings of, 72–73
    targeted by communists, 18–19
causes, worthy and otherwise, v
celibacy, vow of, 29–30
challenge, life without, viii
children, testing their parents, 64
chimpanzees, way better than
        bonobos, 87
chin-ups, 8
Christianity. see also Catholicism
    as foundation of Western
        Civilization, 15–16
chromosomes, X and Y, 80
Church fathers, 16, 27–29
Cicero, 13
clarity, 37, 39, 52
classical education, 18
cleansing
    deep cellular, 44–45
    emotional, 37
collapse
    societal, 40–41
        imminent, 103–104
commitment, 59, 69, 71, 74
communism, 15
    communist subversion, 18–20

confidence
    comes from strength, 4–6
    masculine, necessary, 49
Confucianism, 11
Conner, Janet, quoted, 93
consumerism, the modern religion,
    47
consumption, diseases of, 46–47
contents, supplemental, ix
control, gaining, vi
Cooperstown, New York, 99
couch-lock, 97
Covid lockdowns, 79, 102–103
Create (11th pillar), 109–115
    creation vs. procreation, 109
    faith in the outcome, 115
criticism, fear of, 85–87
crown, symbolism of, 67–68
culture, our degenerate, iv, 99
curiosity, dangers of, 101–102

D

The Dark Knight (movie), 60
deadlift, 6–8, 9
death. see mortality
decisiveness, masculine quality, 79
defiance, as sword and shield, 65
defilement, from social media,
    97–98
Defy (6th pillar), iv, 59–65
    uniquely masculine, 59–60
degeneracy, iii
    last stage of, 53
demons, ii
    better explanation than
        psychology, 29, 46
    do not argue with them, 33–35
    facing one's own, 69
    insidious, or clever?, 111–112
    literal and figurative, 24, 26–
        27, 46
    recognizing you have them,
        37–39
deprecation, by self or others,
    104–106

depression, 39
    and demons, 27, 33
    increased by social media, 25
"The Deputy" (play), 19
detox, book, 15
Devote (7th pillar), v, 67–75
    devotion to family often fails,
        68
    disordered devotion, 71
    everyone is devoted to
        something, 68
        aim at higher things, 71,
            75
        aim at something bigger
            than yourself, 69
dharma, 73
dieting (calorie restriction) vs.
        fasting, 42–44
dips (exercise), 7–8
discipline, 59, 67
discrimination, in reading, 12–13
disempowerment of men, 3
Disney Corporation, 19, 100
dissociative identity disorder, 26
distractions
    many are demonic, 77
    of modern life, 24–25
Divinity School, 11
dream, author's life-changing, vii
drugs, vii, 37–38, 78, 102, 118
dust, we are all, 68, 118–120, 122
dying well, 121–122

E

Eden, Garden of, 32
effeminacy, iii, 24–26, 71–73, 85
    defined by Aquinas, 25
    includes gluttony for
        information, 14–15
    includes indecisiveness, 79
    not the same as femininity, 24
    opposite of perseverance,
        24–26
ego
    calming it, 37

ego-driven goals, 92–93
emasculation, 3
Emerson, Ralph Waldo, 11–13
    his guidelines for reading,
        12–13
emotionality, vii
endocrine disruptors, 56
energy, wasted, 88
epilepsy, 46
estrogen, 50–51
    in tap water, 56
exercises, four best, 6–8
experts
    misplaced faith in, 79
    stupidly recommend living like
        bonobos, 87

F

faith
    blind, is amazing, 115
    necessity of, 70–71
    vs. logic and reason, 70–71
family, 120–121
    author's, vii, 3, 40, 71, 88–91
    often falls apart, 68
    psychodynamics of, 61–62
    targeted by communists, 18
fapping, 20–21, 87
Farmer's Carries (exercise), i
farming, ii
Fast (4th pillar), 28, 37–47
    24 hours best to start with,
        39–40
    40 days (Jesus), 93
    72 hours best in long run,
        41–42
    and prayers, 46
    before setting soul goals, 93
    fasting vs. dieting (calorie
        restriction), 42–44
    history of, 45–47
    not just for weight-loss, 37
    prideful fasting, 39
    purifies the body, sharpens the
        mind, 47

required of students by ancient
philosophers, 47
fat
and testosterone, 52
vs. muscles, burning, 42–44
father, meaning of, 79–80
FDA (Food and Drug
Administration), 41
feminine side, getting in touch with
one's, 38
feminism, 15, 21, 106
a cancer on the planet, 105
does not work, 49–50
feminist teachers, iii
no one remembers feminists,
121
waters down masculinity, 30
5X5 (training program), 8–9
Florida, vii, 4, 23
fluidity, in action, 89
football, author's experience of, 70
frailties, bringing them to the
surface, 39
frailty, and testosterone, 52–53
freaking out, avoiding, 40–41
front squats (exercise), 7–8
Fung, Dr. Jason, 44

G

gardens
Eden, 32
Gethsemane, 35
your own, 120–121
gaslighting, by mainstream, iv–v
Gates, Bill, not an alpha male, 5–6
generations
and generativity, 110
millennials, 53, 69
X, Y, and Z, 53
Genghis Khan, 122
Gethsemane, Garden of, 35
giving vs. taking, 111
globalist scam, 73
gluttony for information, 14, 101
glycogen, 43

goals
ego-driven, 92
troll vs. soul, 91–93
God
as Creator, 79–81
being one's own God, 92
let God do what God does,
92–94, 110–111
like a good coach, challenges
you, 34
the slap of, 78
the ultimate cause, 69–72
Trump is not a god, 118
vs. the material world as
mother, 79–81
you will have one, 117
godlessness, 110–111
Google, 101
grace, in action, 89
great things, inevitably denigrated,
85–87
Greece, ancient, and Greek studies,
11
Guard (10th pillar), 97–107
gymnasium, distractions of, 100,
103
gynocentrism, iii, 80

H

hair, long, vii
halo, a symbolic crown, 67–68
happiness and comfort, life is not
about, 120–121
hard times, coming after Generation
Z, 53
Harvard University, 11
health, as an instrument in the
sumphony of life, 57
heart health, and testosterone, 52
heaven, deserving, 120
highlighter
author's gold, 13
highlight trigger phrases, 94
Hinduism, 11, 16
hippies, 38

Hippocrates, quoted, 46
history
    African vs. European, 16–18
    real vs. fake, 18–19
holiness, many cringe at the word,
    98–99
holiness, wholeness, wholesomeness,
    and integrity, 98–99
Hollywood, 49, 114
homeschooling, vii
homesteading, vii
honesty, armor of the soul, 83
honor, 59
Hooters, 30
hormones, 41–43, 56–57
    affected by pornography, 97
    male and female, 50–51
horse riding, ii
hospices and hospitals, 119
hot flashes, 51
house vs. home, 109
Hulu, 102
hunting, ii, 2
hurricanes, 4, 23

I

Idaho, 89
idols, false, 118–119
Ignatius. see also Brianchaninov,
    Ignatius
    author's middle name, 28
immune system, 41, 45
Indian affairs, reports on, 11
information, too much, 101–2
inspiration, 115
Instagram, ii, 14, 25, 30, 97103
    author's page, 28, 49
insulin, 41, 99
integrity, structural and spiritual, 99
integrity, wholeness, wholesomeness,
    and holiness, 98–99
intersexual dynamics, importance
    of, 20
Iron John (Bly), 61–62
Isaac the Syrian, Saint, quoted,
    33–34

J

Jackson, Michael, 82
James, LeBron, 3
jealousy and envy, encouraged by
    social media, 97
Jesus Christ, 11, 46–47, 72
    fasted for 40 days, 93
    quoted, 86
Jesus Prayer, 35
Jordan, Michael, 89
judging yourself, avoid, 33

K

KGB, 19
King Initiation program, iv, vi, 21
King of Making Men Strong, vii,
    127
king, inner, vi
knowledge, spiritual vs. worldly, 102
Kremlin's campaign of ideological
    subversion, 18–19

L

Latin studies, 11
legacy, spiritual vs. physical, 121
leisure time, and guilt, 88
Leonardo da Vinci, 80–81
liberation, sexual, 100–101
library, 13
Lift (1st pillar), i, 1–9, vI
    lifting and testosterone, 57
liver, role in fasting and dieting, 43
Locke, John, 13
lore, hidden, iv
lost, what to do when you are,
    89–91
loyalty, 59
lust, fire of, 30–32

M

Macarius the Great, Saint, quoted,
    31–32
mammon vs. God, 70
marijuana. see drugs
Marine Corps, 73

marriage, only alternative to monk mode, 30
Marunde, Jesse, 121
masculine values, no longer taught, iii
masculinity, traditional, i–iv
    only subject of this book, viii
    requires belief in something higher, 37
    twelve pillars of, iv–vi
masturbation. see fapping
materialism, is not enough, 37
Matisse, Paul, quoted, 115
matriarchy, and bonobos, 87
The Matrix (movie), 20
meat, bought in stores, not grown or hunted, 119
meathead, author just a, 41
media, mass
    aim to distract and upset us, 23–25
    trust the opposite of what they say, 52
meditation, masculine forms of, 28
Mediterranean diet, 46
Memento mori, 119
men
    create what women improve, 109–110
    denigration of, iii
    designed to create, 109
    finding like-minded, iv
    this book written for, vi
    but not all men, vi
menopause, 51
mentors and elders, men need, 60
metabolic states, 43
mind, sluggish, from too much reading, 14
mirror, seeing yourself in, 81–82
mistakes, author's, iii, vii, 37–39, 69, 71–74, 101–102
    helped him write this book, 85
MMA (Mixed Martial Arts), 2
modernism, iii
modest dress, 100–101

Mommy, waiting for, 79
monasteries, 29, 32
money, attracts girls, 5–6
monk mode, 29–32
monks, 27–32
    seduced by women, 30–32
mortality
    denied by the modern world, ii, 117
    need to face it, 117, 123
Moses, 122
mother, meaning of, 80
movies, 102–103, 114
Muhammad, Prophet, 46
muscles
    and testosterone, 52
    vs. fat, burning, 42–44
    women attracted to, 5–6
music, 77, 102
mythology, Norse, 11

N

narcissism, 26
nature
    becoming one with, 91
    man's fallen, 26, 77
Nazism, falsely attributed to Pope Pius XII, 19
Neo (movie character), 20
Netflix, 102–103
neuroticism, 118
New Age, ii, 37–38, 44, 111
news, half of it is lies, 23–24
newspapers, to be avoided, 12
Nietzsche, Friedrich, quoted, 14
no, saying, 63–64
notebook, for setting soul goals, 93–94

O

occult, the, 37–38
old age, dangers of, 5
Optimize (5th pillar), v, 49–57
organize your life for what is important, 117

Orthodox Church
    Eastern, 28
    Greek, 46
outrage porn, 24
overthinking, dangers of, 33–34

P

pain, life without, viii
patriarchy
    and chimpanzees, 87
    and patterns and fathers, 79
    and the Abrahamic religions,
        15–16
    and the Church fathers, 28
pedophiles and homosexuals in the
    Catholic hierarchy, 72
perseverance, defined by Aquinas,
    25–26
personality types, two bad ones,
    104–105
pheromones, 6
pills. see also red pill (concept)
    birth control, 50–51
        and tap water, 56
Pius XII, Pope, 19
plastic, in water bottles, dangers
        of, 56
Plato, 47
pleasure-seeking, effeminate, 14–15
    unwillingness to give up, 24–25
Plutarch, quoted, 46–47
polarity, sexual, 5–6, 52
political correctness, 2, 29, 73
popes
    Francis a communist, 72
    Pius XII not a Nazi, 19
pornography, 21, 30–31, 87, 97,
        126
posture, 5–8
potential, living up to your, 86–87
pothole analogy for fasting, 44
power, God-given, iv
prayers, 28, 32
    and fasting, 48
    better than arguing with
        demons, 33–35

Jesus Prayer, 35
    personal mantra, 36
Pressfield, Steven, quoted, 111
pride
    encouraged by social media, 97
    in fasting, 39
    in not knowing latest pop
        culture, 103
    in reading, 14–15
programming, by popular culture,
        102–104
promiscuity, 50–51
provider, man as, 2
psychics, 37
psychology, 26
    dependence on, 79
pushback, author's extreme, v, 50
pyramids and skyscrapers, 109

R

The Rational Male (Tomassi), 21
Read (2nd pillar), 11–21
    active vs. passive reading,
        12–13
    can be taken to excess, 14–15
    deeply and widely, 11
    history of the West, 15–17
    reading is the gym of the mind,
        21
    vocational reading, 20–21
real world, dissociation from,
        increased by social media,
        25
reason and logic vs. faith, 70–71
red pill (concept), 15, 20–21, 28
    blue pill, 20, 28, 49
research, babies don't, 113
resilience, and testosterone, 52–53
resistance (to doing your work)
    as guide to what you should do,
        112–113
    demonic, 111–112
    in setting soul goals, 94
    toxic, 111
respect, earning, vi
responsibility, always lies with the

strongest, 3–4
Reveal (8th pillar), v, 77–83
revelations
    may be ugly, 78
    start from right in front
        of you, 77–78
rhetoric, 11
risk taking, and testosterone, 53
rock bottom, as turning point, 78
Rome, ancient, 11, 122
rulers, men as natural, 3

S

sadomasochism, 26
sanctity and work, life is about, 120
Satan, 28, 32
scientists, misplaced faith in, 79
seasons of the year, 45
seasons, life happens in, 86
self-aggrandizement and self-
        deprecation, 104
self-reliance, 11–12
"Self-Reliance" (Emerson), 11
self-worship, 111
sexual confidence, and testosterone,
        48, 53
sexual revolution, 99–101
shadow, seeing your own, 82
shame, 62–64, 81–82
shipwreck, danger in a woman's
        face, 31
silence, 35
skull on desk, as reminder of
        mortality, 119
sleep, and testosterone, 57
sloth, 34
    encouraged by social media, 97
social media
    avoid, 14, 97
    likes are irrelevant, 110
    not the real world, 25
society, our degenerate, i, 63
soul goal statement, 94
soul goals, 93–94
soul, cannot die, 120
Soviet Union, 19

sperm counts, dropping, 54
spirituality, 37
    and devotion, 67–68
sports, "the zone," and grace, 89
status and attraction, 5–6
stillness, 27–28, 35
stoicism, 26
Stop (3rd pillar), 23–35
strength
    as foundation, 9
    as guiding beacon, 75
    as masculine competence, 2–3
    four best exercises for building,
        6–8
    full-body, v
    not just for young men, 5
    not living up to your, 1
    physical vs. mental and
        spiritual, ii
strength training
    builds confidence, 4–5
    recommended programs, 9
strongman, author's experience as,
        i, v
stubbornness
    as a virtue, 114–115
    vs. resilience and vigilance, 115
stupidity, as a virtue, 113–114
survival course, 89–91
sword and shield
    defiance as, 65
    symbolism of, 60–61
symphony, life as a, 57

T

taking vs. giving, 111
Taoism, 16
teachers, feminist, iii
television, 102–04
testosterone, ii, v, 2, 5, 49–57
    9 benefits of, 55–53
    9 symptoms of low T, 55
    demonization of, 51
    levels dropping
        not just in older men, 54
        surely orchestrated, 49

your levels need testing, 55
thyroid, 42
Tiger King (Netflix series), 103
TikTok, 14, 97
Tomassi, Rollo, quoted, 21
trigger phrases, in setting soul goals,
    94
troll goals, 91–92
Trump, Donald J., 49
    possibly God-guided, definitely
        not a god, 118
    "Trust your dick," not a good
        motto, 100
trusting in God, 79–81
21 Convention, 68

U

utopia, not achievable, 70

V

validation, waiting for, is sinful, 113
video games, 21
Vigano, Archbishop, 72–73
vigilance, importance of, 24, 26, 35,
    100–101, 104, 107
villain, OK to be one, 60
vocation, dig into it, 20–21

W

walls
    importance of, 59–60
    space inside them is feminine,
        59–60
The War of Art (Pressfield), quoted,
    111–112
warrior
    being a, 67
    lives set off from society, 69, 71
    whistleblower warriors, 72–74
warrior child, 61–62
water filters, 56
water, and testosterone, 56
WebMD, v
weight, troubles of the world as, 1
Western Civilization, founded on

Christianity, 15–16
whistleblower warriors, 72–74
white knighting, does not work,
    49–50
wholeness, wholesomeness, holiness,
    and integrity, 98–99
wilderness, being lost in the, 89–91
willpower, and testosterone, 53
wisdom, lost, iv
women
    and perennial diets, 42
    avoidance of, 28–33
    improve what men create,
        109–110
    more physical than men, 121
    now outpacing men in every
        realm, 105–106
    this book not written for, vi
    virtues of, 59–60
    want powerful men, 104–105
    what they say vs. what they do,
        5–6
    will never be as strong as men,
        2–3
work and sanctity, life is about, 120
work, necessity of, 120–121
world
    cannot be saved, 122
    our atheistic, 16, 81
    our degenerate, ii, 11, 99, 118
    this fallen, 65, 68
Writing Down Your Soul (Conner),
    93

Y

"You only live once," not a good
    motto, 100
YouTube, vii, 7, 38, 48, 60, 69, 85,
    92, 101, 113–114

Z

Zen Buddhism, 16, 27
zombie apocalypse, 40–41
"the zone," in sports, 89
Zoroastrianism, 11
Zusha, Rabbi, 122–123

Made in United States
North Haven, CT
21 March 2024